EASILY CREATE HYPNOTIC OFFERS FOR ANYTHING

I've Used This One Marketing Technique To Raise Over $2,000,000 Crafting Undeniably Irresistible Offers On The Internet..And I'll Teach You To Do It Too.

Piyush Agarwal

SEO ORB Digital Solutions

CONTENTS

Title Page   1

Copyright   2

Stop Risking Your Valuable Time, Effort and Money on Ineffective Marketing...   5

Easily Create Hypnotic Offers For Anything!   6

What Is This Guide About And Why You Should Read It NOW   8

WHY should you listen to me?   14

Section 1 - How triggering your prospects' BUYING emotions can dramatically INCREASE your profits!   16

How To "Build a Bond" With Your Reader Within Seconds   17

How To Effortlessly Persuade Your Readers   25

How To Instantly Eliminate Your Competitors   30

How To Get A Prospect To Do (Almost) Anything You Want   34

Consider Adding a SALES VIDEO to Your Offer!   40

Lead With Your USP   43

SECTION II - Secrets To Creating Powerfully Persuasive Sales Copy   50

The One Super-Explosive Technique That You Can Use To Blow Up Your Conversions   53

How to Build Perceived Value With Images and Illustration   57

Without This, Your Sales Will Plummet   61

How To Create POWERFUL Headlines / Titles That Virtually Force Your Prospects To Read Your Complete   63

How To Get The Greatest Copywriters To Write Your Copy For FREE!   75

A Neat Trick That Will Make Your Sales Copy SING!   78

A STUPID-SIMPLE Way To Build Tremendous PERCEIVED Value In All Your Offers!   80

Turn Your Guarantee Into a VALUABLE BENEFIT!   83

How To Light A FIRE Under The Buyers' Butt, So They Buy NOW!   85

How To Draw Your Reader Into Your Copy?   86

Something That Will Increase Your Conversion Rates Even With Mediocre Sales Copy   92

Yet Another Powerful Way To Build Even MORE, Perceived Value!   95

How To Write So Even SKIM READERS Are Drawn Into Your Sales Copy And Converted Into BUYERS!   98

A SUPER SIMPLE Way to Differentiate Yourself From The Competition   102

An Easy Way To Get Readers To Believe You Completely   106

How To Increase Sales By Offering More Choices   110

BONUS SECTION   114

How To POWERFULLY Tap Into People's Emotional Buying Triggers   115

A Simple Tip To Increase Sales   126

How To Adapt Your Copy For Email, Social Media Posts, Product Review Pages, and Self-Published Amazo   128

From Blank Page To Completed Promo Creating Hypnotic Offers Step-by-Step   137

Here's How I Go From A Blank Page To A Completed Written Promo   141

STOP RISKING YOUR VALUABLE TIME, EFFORT AND MONEY ON INEFFECTIVE MARKETING…

EASILY CREATE HYPNOTIC OFFERS FOR ANYTHING!

I've Used This One Marketing Technique To Raise Over $2,000,000 Crafting Undeniably Irresistible Offers On The Internet..And I'll Teach You To Do It Too..Even If You Can't Write and Haven't Got A Single Creative Bone In Your Body…

Enjoy Success At Last!

You Can Now…

- Use This Simple, Step-by-step System To Turn All Your Offers Into Powerful Money Makers - 100% GUARANTEED!
- Create an army of hungry loyal buyers, improve repeat sales, increase the dollar amount of every sale and double or even triple your profits in record time.
- Do all this YOURSELF, without having to hire an expensive copywriter or marketer.

Practical, Proven and Time Tested "Marketing Technique" Guaranteed To Increase The Net Income of Any Business Almost Instantly!

WHAT IS THIS GUIDE ABOUT AND WHY YOU SHOULD READ IT NOW

This book reveals the **insider secrets of persuasion.**

You'll learn how to <u>Create Hypnotic Offers for ANYTHING!</u>

The power to persuade with only words can change your life! Whether

- You are promoting your own products or services.
- You are promoting/reviewing affiliate products.
- You are promoting eBay, Amazon, Etsy or Fiverr products.
- You are building an email list.
- You are growing a Facebook Group / Page.
- You are writing book descriptions for self-published books.
- You are promoting your physical products, books, info products, or anything else...

Never again will you stare at a blank page wondering what to write or how to persuade. SUCCESS online will be yours because you will BE ABLE TO PERSUADE with ONLY YOUR WORDS.

We will be covering many persuasion tactics in this book. HERE'S YOUR FIRST SECRET.

People are always trying to **move away from pain** or **move towards pleasure**. To make ANY product promo "irresistible"... **The pleasure (or benefit) of buying your offer should far outweigh the pain of parting with money.**

You must OVERLOAD them with perceived value!

The keyword is "perceived value" and not "actual value."

You may have the greatest products in the world at the most unbelievable prices, but if you fail to communicate the "perceived value" to the reader, it's all in vain. They won't buy it. **We must COMMUNICATE that value!**

This book will show you how.

It's not enough to HAVE value... we must demonstrate that value to potential buyers in a way that gets them to "take immediate action" and buy. **That's what this book is all about...** Showing you how you can EASILY create offers that (no matter what the product) people will ACT ON IMMEDIATELY!

Is this just another copywriting book?

Yes and No.

I will discuss copywriting, sure. But this book is not just a list of rules on how to write copy, like most copywriting books are.

For your copy to be compelling, **you need to understand BUYER PSYCHOLOGY**. You need to CONNECT with the reader and get them EXCITED about your offer. **This book helps you do just that!**

If you are going to teach someone how to drive a car, you wouldn't just tell them to get behind the wheel and step on the gas, right?

You would likely first acquaint them with the rules of the road. Show them what a red light means vs. a green light and what a solid center line means vs. a dashed line, right?

Likewise, **this book has TWO main sections**. The 1st section is titled, **"How Triggering Your Prospects' BUYING Emotions Can Dramatically Increase Your Profits"** and it nose-dives into the specific psychology of what makes people buy and shows you how you can **increase your sales effortlessly, even with an average copy.**

In other words, there is much more to creating persuasive offers than just good copywriting. Your relationship with your prospect, your USP (Unique Selling Position), and even your BONUSES or how you state your Guarantee ALL play into adding PERCEIVED VALUE to your offer (whatever the offer is - an affiliate product, a service, an Amazon/eBay Listing, a self-published Amazon Book, or anything).

We cover ALL of this in section I in easy to follow bite-size pieces. **Don't worry...** It's simpler than it sounds!

In the 2nd section of this book, **"Secrets To Creating Powerfully Persuasive Sales Copy That Will Earn You MORE Money With Less Traffic,"** you'll discover how to write compelling sales copy that converts prospects into buyers by the truck load.

You will never have to pay someone hundreds of dollars to write a sales letter or promo piece. And as said, Never again will you stare at a blank page not knowing where to start or what to write.

I will show you how to increase your conversion rates significantly, so you get **MORE SALES with FEWER PROSPECTS**.

Remember, the PURPOSE of any sales copy is to get people to BUY (or take some action such as sign up for your email list, or even to get a click). That's it!

You can have the most fantastic product(s) in the world and tons of prospects, but if your offer doesn't turn skeptical viewers into raving customers and does so in substantially good numbers, you will starve (even if your competition's products are inferior).

If you indulge me for a moment, consider this...

Back in the mid-'70s, **Sony came out with a recording format called Betamax.**
Around the same time, **JVC released an alternative format they called VHS.**

Which format was the better one?

Betamax.

Ask any old-time video aficionado, and they'll tell you.

And which one did the market choose?

The VHS.

Now, why do you think that happened?

Sony failed to connect with the market. It couldn't communicate the benefits of its format to prospective buyers.

People were just not convinced that Betamax would provide better value for money.
And so, Betamax just faded away.

Sony's failure was its inability to communicate the superior value of its product to the average consumer (in an exciting way), so VHS, an inferior product, succeeded!

ALSO, the power to "persuade effectively" virtually ALWAYS wins over price!

My point here is that having 'good,' 'awesome,' or even the most 'explosive' products is not going to cut it anymore... we must craft our "product offers" to deliver the value of our goods in an exciting way that sets us apart from our competition and makes the decision to buy, as said, a 'no brainer.'

Before you move on, you may have noticed I talked about showing you how to increase your 'conversion rate'.

If you don't know what that is, or why that's important, here goes:

Conversion rate is, say, how many buyers you win per 100 visitors. It's a key ROI (Return On Investment) metric. **The higher your conversion rate, the more efficient your marketing becomes.**

For example, say your current product offer page is converting at 2.5% (that is, 5 buyers per 200 visitors). If with a few tweaks we can get the page converting at 10%, that's 20 buyers per 200 visitors.
In other words, you're making **4X the profit from the SAME LEVEL OF TRAFFIC.**

Does that sound like something you should try out?

> NOTE: If you have any questions, comments, or feedback, email me at p@seoorb.com (my email and not an auto-responder).

One quick note before we Get Started...

"Persuasion is a powerful love potion. Use it wisely."

By the end of this book, you will be able to craft explosively hypnotic, and jaw-dropping product offers.

DO NOT USE YOUR POWERS FOR MANIPULATION.

Be like a SUPERHERO... Use your "powers" for GOOD, not evil.

Ask yourself this...

"If this visitor was my Grandma,
Will I sell my product/offer to her?
Will I be proud of what I am offering her?
Will my product solve her problem?"

If the answer is a profound "YES!" then you're okay!! (if not, then you should rethink your offer).

WHY SHOULD YOU LISTEN TO ME?

Okay...So why should you listen to me? Well, because I'm a really nice guy...Oh, and also...

My offers, including affiliate offers, my own product and services, and other people's offers that I've written copy for have raked in $2,146,159 (and counting) in Sales Revenue in the last two years! (even though I don't maintain my own email list and I don't have any affiliates).

One of my promotions in the Entertainment Niche for a client did over **$200K in revenue in less than six months from just two traffic sources.**

Another one from the **Corporate Team Building and HR space** reached **1825.4% return on ad-spend.**

And also, I come from a marketing background. I have been in direct sales and marketing for over ten years. (If you want to create super persuasive offers, you can do direct sales and marketing for 10+ years, or just follow this guide).

SECTION 1 - HOW TRIGGERING YOUR PROSPECTS' BUYING EMOTIONS CAN DRAMATICALLY INCREASE YOUR PROFITS!

HOW TO "BUILD A BOND" WITH YOUR READER WITHIN SECONDS

*That Will Make
Them MUCH More Likely To Buy!*

This following is magical. Persuasion is about more than just good copywriting. We will cover good copywriting secrets in section II of this guide, BUT let me ask you a question. Wouldn't it be nice if we could get HIGH 10% 20% 25% conversions even with mediocre sales copy? We Can! Read On…

Here's the first part of this magic method… Always, always, always remember that People Buy on Emotion! To attain real long term success online, we have to "personally connect" with our prospects on an emotional level. We need to build CREDIBILITY, LIKEABILITY, LOYALTY, and TRUST with our prospects. **We do this by building kinship with them.** (Don't worry -- it's easy to do! Keep reading).

To sum up, building a personal connection with our viewers by itself goes a long way towards boosting conversions.

It sets us apart from other marketers, and makes the viewers feel part of an exclusive tribe, which is a powerful motivator for them to check out our offer!

Fortunately, as we shall see, this is easier than it seems.

Now don't be intimidated! Relationship building is **simple...** The mistake people make is they overcomplicate it!!

Quickly building a relationship is not only *possible. In fact, it is a must.*

Let me digress for a moment AND TALK about "direct sales" a bit (and then I'll show you how to adapt what we learn to written promotions)

To see how fast relationship building works, let's look at **Trisha, a 'sales rep' of a local retail store that sells beauty products**.

Trisha's job was to assist people in selecting the right skincare products. The job paid 100% incentive or minimum wage, whichever was more. Trisha certainly wasn't there for minimum wage! She was earning four times what other sales reps were making, because she was GOOD at her job (persuading people and making them happy in the process). She also didn't act like a typical "commission" salesperson!

I'm sure you have had an experience of walking into a store with commission salespeople and 'being pounced' upon by half a dozen wide-eyed "representatives" rushing at you before you can even catch your breath. I used to call it **"running the gauntlet."**

What these salespeople are doing wrong is trying to vie for your business before they've built any kind of relation or kinship with you... And of course, your instinct is to rebel and become defensive, skeptical, and distrusting (precisely the OPPOSITE of what marketers need to accomplish!).

T did it differently... She wouldn't stand upfront with all the other 'ready to pounce' salespeople... She'd hang back at the store "dusting" and looking busy, BUT she would watch the parking lot for approaching customers... As T saw a family or couple approaching, she would casually "dust" her way to the front of the store and just "happen" to arrive at the store's front door at the same time as the arriving family... She would open the door for them with a genuine smile and say, "Hi, come on in... Welcome to [store]", and then T would step back to give them lots of room! (the opposite of "pouncing").

Since she made "first verbal contact," they were considered (by store rules) to now be her customers and so there was no "gauntlet."

At this point a typical sales person would pummel the customer with "qualifying questions" to "lead them to a specific product."

But not T. She'd say, "have a look around, take your time, because at our store, looking is FREE... If you have any questions, just ask (smile) my name is Trisha", and then... (SALES GOD FORBID!!) she'd move away, leaving the visitor to check out the products at their own pace.

At this stage, it's been maybe a minute or so since the family has entered the store. And within that time, **T has established a relationship with them.**

How did she do that?

By pouncing on them from the get-go? **No.**

By thrusting sales and offers in their face? **No.**

Here's what she did:

- She **made them feel welcome** in the store, and set them at ease.
- She **cracked a joke** about looking at the products being

free, which showed her as an intelligent and good-natured person.

- Finally, she **left them ALONE**, <u>leaving no scope for any suspicion or belligerence.</u>

At this point, the people either ask a question, as in "we're looking for this or that...." Or they will look about and become bewildered with the amount of product selection (this store had a HUGE variety).

Then T continued building on to the relationship... "Is this your 1st time in this store?" .... Well, I can give you a layout.... Would you like a quick layout? ... or a detailed layout?? Then T would give them the layout of the store and which place had what kind of product stocked... and now rather than pepper them with "qualifying questions" T observed towards which part of the store they would move.

And as the customers walked the store, T would chime in another helpful tip, "Oh, by the way, I should tell you about our "4-Week Satisfaction Guarantee Policy' - after today, you will never have to look for new skincare products again....."

See how helpful she is being? See how she is enhancing their experience as a customer at the store? Do they feel like they are getting "sold to" or "being forced to buy"?

T has just built LIKEABILITY, CREDIBILITY, and TRUST in a few minutes, and they haven't even begun talking products yet!

More kinship building takes place throughout the visit but, particularly when it comes to preparing the price quote for their selected products.... That "wait," while the "price" is calculated, is tense for any customer... So, as T is crunching numbers, she says, "Oh hey, nice jacket," or "Oh hey nice broach"... What's the story behind that? And it would get the customer talking and conversing about a story they like to tell (instead of waiting silently in tension).

Another example of building a kinship or making an emotional connection with someone quickly is when trying to aid someone who has just become unexpectedly and severely injured. You don't have a lot of "time" to establish CREDIBILITY and TRUST. Yet paramedics build kinship routinely.

"Hi, I'm [name], I'm a Paramedic, I am going to help you okay? (an empathetic promise is a great way to build an emotional connection.

Think of your last doctor's appointment or medical appointment and how the nurse was… Empathetic, conversational, humorous (if warranted), reassuring, etc. They built a kinship with you within seconds of meeting you.

From the above, we see that we build kinship with someone not by bragging about our product (at least not initially) but by making a positive emotional connection or BOND with our prospect. We can do this by…

- Empathizing with them
- Showing them we understand their problem BEFORE talking about products
- Asking open-ended questions
- Showing some personality
- Validating them
- Making a promise to help them (whether or not they buy)…

We will get into specifics in a flash, but remember this…

People will NEVER remember what you said, but they will NEVER forget how you made them FEEL - it's the same with your OFFER.

If your product presentation makes your prospective buyer <u>feel good, feel respected, feel intelligent, feel comfortable, feel listened to, feel validated</u>, and SATISFIES THEIR CRAVINGS, they will excitedly buy from you… again and again..and again.

Now I realize you can't ask your reader to answer questions, but you can still make a personal connection with your readers by asking questions in your copy!

What if we had a sales page or email promo that asked one or more of the following?

- "What if I show you exactly how to do _______ even if you DON'T buy my book today?" (helping them whether or not they buy)
- "Are you tired of false promises? Me too..." (validation)
- Wouldn't it be nice if..." (open-ended question)
- "Have you ever dreamt of a world where...." (open-ended question)
- "Are you tired of people dumber than you being richer than you?" (validation)
- "What qualities would your perfect soulmate have?" (open-ended question)

We can also use empathizing statements that validate our customers' problem....

- "If you have trouble with _______, you're not alone."
- "If you have trouble talking to women, I've been there too."
- "If you've failed in the past at _______, it's not your fault."

(more on this later)

We can even use open-ended questions to bypass a person's skepticism! For example, if we say, <u>"This book shows you step by step how to find your soulmate</u>," the prospect might be skeptical of that claim. BUT if instead, we say, <u>"Wouldn't it be nice if there was a simple step by step way anyone could find their soulmate?"</u>

See how a simple tweak can boost your sales process? The content of the message remains the same. All you did was change the form in which you presented it.

We are now getting the prospect to IMAGINE with no skeptical filters on...They are becoming "emotionally invested" in what we have to say and what we are offering! They are more accepting of our claim as we are asking them to "imagine" it, not "evaluate" it.

Another way to connect emotionally with our prospects is this... Rather than speaking of our product in objective third-person terms (this product slices tomatoes fast), **we speak of our product in personal terms** (With this product, you'll be slicing tomatoes faster than even... I know I am!)

We could say this... "if you're anything like me, you HATE slicing tomatoes because it's slow and the slices come out all crooked".... Finding common ground with your prospect is a great way to seed and nurture a relationship!

Rather than saying, "This camera eliminates 'red eye' automatically," try this, "With this camera, I never have to worry about awkward red eye...and neither will you...the camera eliminates 'red eye' automatically". See how we turned 'red eye' form a mere annoyance to an emotional awkwardness?

Here's another example...

"This painting breathes life into our dull living room. It's such a delight to look at, and a great conversation starter when we have friends and family over. And we continually receive admiring comments from visitors as well!... so will you!"

By putting the product features into PERSONAL and EMOTIONAL terms, you connect with the prospect quickly.

Look through your copy... anywhere you see words like "it," "this," or "the," try to replace them with the terms "I," "you," and "your." Also, try to convert any third-person reference to 1st person.

For example... consider this statement....
"This guide shows the ways anyone can make a personal con-

nection with <u>their</u> prospects. <u>It</u> goes into the easy to understand details...."

As compared to this...

"In <u>your</u> guide, <u>I</u> show <u>you</u> ten ways <u>you</u> can make a personal connection with <u>your</u> viewer. <u>I</u> make the details easy to understand..." **See the difference?**

HOW TO EFFORTLESSLY PERSUADE YOUR READERS

By Simply Restating Their Feeling and Opinions

Before creating your offer, think about what people interested in your product would want. What would be their 'pet peeves'? What would they consider to be important? What are their passions? How would they feel about certain issues? What are their beliefs?

Then….echo those feelings, opinions, beliefs, and passions in your offers!

By validating your prospects' pet peeves, fears, objections, opinions, beliefs, feelings, and desires you make the offer relatable thereby creating a strong bond of credibility, likeability, and trustworthiness.

Let's see these two features - **validation and being relatable** - in action.

Consider the following headline:

**If You Haven't Made A Single Dime Online Yet,
It's Not Your Fault!** (validation)
**Unemployed Husband Cracks Code And Makes $427 with No
List and NO Website with just 3 Hours 'Work'!** (relatable)

The first line validates the prospect's pain point, and reaches out to them emotionally. The second one offers a third-party example that the prospect can relate to.

This will transform into more sales, even with a sub-par sales copy!

For another example, let's pick a unique niche. Suppose we have a blog in the kids' bicycling niche… and we are doing a review of Amazon Bicycle helmets. Kids' bicycling helmets retail on Amazon for anywhere between $50 - $70 each, or more, so they would return a nice affiliate commission per sale.

Before we start writing our blog reviews; however, <u>we should first think about what people who buy kids' bicycle helmets would "believe in."</u> It would be pretty safe to conclude that any parent looking for a "bicycle helmet for their child" would believe in <u>keeping their child/children as safe as possible</u>… right? At the same time, they want to let kids be kids and "have fun!"

What else?

Well, from reading reviews on Amazon, we see that people also consider weight and ventilation necessary. They like "lightweight" yet durable helmets that allow for proper ventilation in addition to providing head protection. They also value easily adjustable straps.

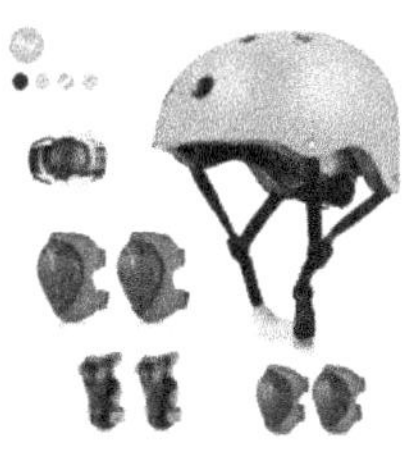

Sponsored
MTUBTB Children's Bicycle Helmet, Toddler's Helmet, Kids Protective Gear and 3-12-Year-Old Boys Girls Adjustable Sports Protection...

$29⁹⁹
Save 5% with coupon (some sizes/colors)

Sponsored
Binggoooo Kids Bike Helmet CPSC Certified Children Multi-Sport Adjustable Helmet for Girls Boys

$21⁹⁹

Sponsored
Anharluka Toddler Kids Bike Helmet

$27⁹⁹
Save 5% with coupon (some sizes/colors)

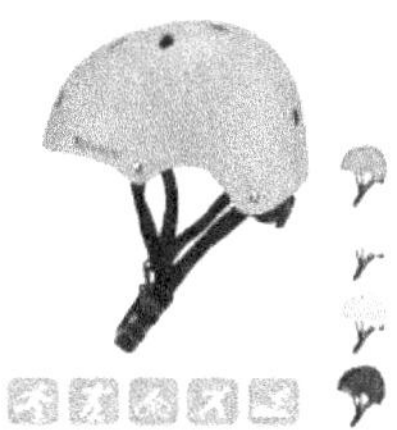

Sponsored
TOURNOW Kids Bike and Skateboard Helmet, 11 Air Vents Adjustable Dial Helmet for Rollerblading Skateboard Cycling Skating Bike Scooter

$19⁹⁹
Only 12 left in stock - order soon.

M Merkapa Kids Bike Helmet Adjustable 3D Shark Bicycle Helmets for Toddler and Youth

$14⁹⁹

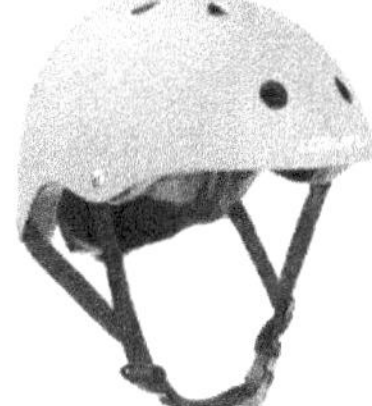

LERUJIFL Kids Helmet Adjustable from Toddler to Youth Size, Ages 3 to 8 Years Old Boys Girls Multi-Sports Safety Cycling Skating Scooter...

$26⁹⁵

Exclusky Kids Bike Helmets Lightweight Adjustable Bicycle Cycling Helmet for Boys Girls 50-57cm (Ages 5-13)

$36⁹⁹

Schwinn Thrasher Bike Helmet, Lightweight Microshell Design, Sizes for Adults, Youth and Children

$24⁹⁹
More Buying Choices
$22.25 (4 used & new offers)

NOTE: You **can minimize guesswork and understand what your customers value** by looking at:
- Feedback to competitor's offers
- Facebook Fan Pages/groups in the niche
- Searching forums to see what people are asking/saying
- Checking the titles and table or contents of the hottest books in your niche
- or (as we did here) going to Amazon and reading product reviews.

I'll go into more detail on this in a later section.

<u>Now within your product reviews (or in an introduction to them), you can make a personal connection with this market by</u>

<u>echoing their feelings, opinions, passions, and beliefs...</u> Imagine a kids' bike helmet description that opens like this....

"As a parent, I love letting my child have fun while getting healthy exercise too while riding her bike. **BUT I am always worried about her getting hurt!** If you believe, as I do, in keeping your children as safe as possible and also enjoy getting the best value for your hard-earned dollars, you're going to LOVE what I found! *With these kids' helmets, I feel a lot better, knowing my child is safer and as fully protected as possible.*

See how we've built kinship with our viewer by using common beliefs? WE BOTH enjoy seeing our child/children have fun, we BOTH believe in keeping our children as safe as possible, and we BOTH want to get the best value for our hard-earned dollars.

Ahhhh! Yes, you say, but Piyush.... What if I don't have any children? How can I bond then?

No problem.... Try this...

If, as a parent, you love seeing your child have fun while getting healthy exercise riding her bike. **BUT, like any parent, you are also always worried about them getting hurt too** AND *if you believe, as I do, in keeping children as safe as possible* (and also getting the best value for your hard-earned dollar). You are going to LOVE what I've found! With any of these helmets, I feel a lot better, knowing children are as fully protected as possible!

As you can see, in a second example, we echo and share our viewer's beliefs even though we don't have children.

Notice ALSO how we haven't begun talking about the specifics of the product(s), and yet already have built trust, credibility, likeability, and DESIRABILITY, etc.

Also, in the examples above, we use the 1st person and words like "I," "you," and "your" wherever possible.

Here is another example of echoing your prospect's beliefs. "If you believe like I do. that your home should mirror your unique personality, you're going to love this."

See how we've established an emotional common ground with our viewer in a personal way before they even know what the product is?

The intro above could be the lead-in for many different products! (paintings, statues, cookware, table lamps, candle holders, pillows, curtains, plumbing fixtures, ceiling fans, etc.)

Also by tying our offers to our prospects' CORE BELIEFS, it will make it almost impossible for them to turn down the offer as that will be a violation of their belief system… People will start to talk themselves into saying a YES!

I remember one product sales page for a money-making business plan (years ago) that had pretty mediocre sales copy but ended with the line….

 <u>"You May Never Be A Millionaire, But After Today, You'll Never Be Able To Say No One Gave You The Chance To Be A Millionaire."</u>

That line strongly echoed my belief that my success or failure rests with ME and me alone and not with others…. I bought the book! (and no I'm still not a millionaire, but I learned a lot from it).

HOW TO INSTANTLY ELIMINATE YOUR COMPETITORS

POOF!

Wouldn't it be nice to have ZERO competition? You could charge higher prices, get more buyers, and not worry about what other people in your niche are offering! Here's the secret....

NOTE: See how I presented the claim "zero competition" as a question to reduce skepticism? .... okay, back to it....

<u>You can create even more "perceived value" for your visitors by differentiating yourself from your competition, to the point where they become irrelevant!</u>

You can easily differentiate yourself in any number of ways (and it doesn't have to be expensive or complicated either!)

For example, find something missing from all the similar products in your niche and ADD it to yours. OR, find something that your competition isn't doing (or not saying), and DO IT and SAY IT!

If it's an affiliate product, add something to it for when people purchase through your link! (more on this below).

In the kids' bicycle helmet example above, you could say, "I showed this bicycle helmet to an ER MD, and he agreed that it was a great value for the following reasons..."

Imagine WHAT CREDIBILITY THAT WOULD GIVE TO YOUR PROMO OR REVIEW (that your competition lacks!)

<u>Interviews with industry-experts</u> (or excerpts from interviews) are a valuable "extra" to include in your offers to build credibility and trustworthiness as well. <u>Plus, it's an incredible yet easy and 'zero-cost' way to differentiate yourself from your competition.</u>

You could interview the product manufacturer/creator or experts in your niche and existing customers of the product that you are promoting.

Interview an expert or a critic if you are selling artwork.

If you are selling 'How To' Books, you could interview the book creator or other buyers. Alternatively, you could USE the product and do a "case study."

Another way to differentiate yourself with the competition is to offer bonus material on how to use your product efficiently. Simple examples would be "time saving tips", "assembly guide", "other uses for", and so on.

Info like this, contained within your listing or added as a bonus when they purchase (or both!), <u>provides upfront value</u> to your prospects (that your competition lacks). At the same time, it increases the desire for your product(s). All that at little or no additional cost.

For another example, suppose we have a page offering a selection of genuine leather backpacks (yes, AMAZON has these). IF within our review or promo page, we include a sub-blurb on how to clean leather easily, so these backpacks look like they never age, we've just added tremendous perceived value to these backpacks AND hugely differentiated ourselves from any competition!

If we are selling a collector's item and within our listing, we educate our visitor on what to look for to be sure that the thing is genuine and truly valuable, we have not only increased our trustworthiness in the eyes of our viewer but also caused them to DISTRUST competitors! <u>Double whammy!</u>

If you show a "manual" way to do something online and then offer a software product that automates it, you have "built-in" credibility, trust, and value upfront!

The sky is the limit on what types of "value-added info" you can come up with and add to your offers. Differentiating yourself from the competition is particularly important when you are promoting/recommending affiliate products.

Want a simple way to differentiate yourself and crush your competition when promoting affiliate products?

<u>Offer exclusive bonuses</u> related to the affiliate product! For physical products, you can offer a downloadable digital gift with virtually anything valuable on it (related to your product) to make your offer unique, EXCLUSIVE, and extra helpful in your customer's eyes. It can be user tips, maintenance tips, anything!

You could also put together an info package like a PDF bundle or Series of videos, which would not cost you anything and have it delivered to the customer via email / in a flash-drive. That would add tremendous perceived AND actual value to all of your product offerings!

You can even create a resource list in a PDF, which is nothing more than a list of internet links to online resources and tutorials (written/video) related to your product.

Again the sky is your limit.

Speaking of BONUSES, want a way to catapult your positive testimonials and crash your refund rates?

Try including a valuable and thoughtful **unannounced SURPRISE FREE BONUS!**... A bonus you never even disclosed in your offer.

In our cosmetics business, we sell 70% of our products online. Whenever we sell a beauty care product, we include a free 'face wash' with it... We NEVER mention the "face wash" is included in our listing... We just surprise the customer... and we get glowing testimonials and excellent feedback with near-zero refunds!

I ordered a wireless mouse on Amazon. To my surprise, the mouse came with a pack of '6 AAA Batteries', which the listing did not mention. That would have me covered for six months, if not more. The seller incurred very little extra cost in throwing in those batteries, but the gesture was enough to get a ~~good~~ great review from me.

Again, at the risk of sounding repetitive and redundant, imagination is your only limit.

It need not take a lot of money, time or effort to do these things but they can skyrocket your response rates, bpost customer reviews, and plummet your refund rates (as well as encourage repeat sales!).

I've seen countless examples of affiliates outselling the product creator, simply because of their bonuses!

HOW TO GET A PROSPECT TO DO (ALMOST) ANYTHING YOU WANT

And THANK You For It!

No, it's not by hypnotism.

To create compelling product offers or recommendations that your visitors will act on and BUY (**plus** not demand a refund, plus give you great reviews), you need to identify your prospects' emotional triggers, a.k.a. "hot spots", and capitalize on them.

It's easier to do than you think!

To figure out your prospects' "hotspots", look at testimonials and reviews for similar products. You can use places like **Facebook groups**, **niche forums**, and **Q&A sites** like **Quora** for this research.

If you LOOK & LISTEN long enough, the customer will TELL YOU, what you need to TELL THEM, to get the sale.

Once we know what our customers want, value, and believe in,

it's much easier to create emotional connections with them, validate them, and hit their buying triggers.

So, what kinds of information about your prospects should you look to uncover to put this into action?

Who are you helping?

What do they need help with?

And how can you speak their language in a way that they are going to trust you and pay attention to you?

When you know your prospects at this level of detail, you will be able to create content that makes them go "Without this, I am LOSING out....I better buy".

Your copy, images, graphics, webinars, emails, conversations etc should all mirror your prospect's deep feelings about their situation.

If you 'speak their language', not only will they buy; they will FALL OVER THEMSELVES giving you a good review. Demands for returns and refunds will be a distant memory for you.

If you fail to echo1 their desires, their values, their fears, etc flowing through your content, their reaction will be "Sounds interesting, but is it really for me?". Or worse, "Ugh! Why am I even looking at this?".

The question that remains is: how can you find out all that information about your prospective customers? Especially if you haven't sold anything to them, or dealt with them before?

CASE STUDY: How you can identify your
prospects' 'emotional hotspots'

Whenever I create a new offer or am going after a new market, I start by finding my ideal prospect or my perfect customer on Facebook and then go and find and learn as much as I can about them.

For the purposes of this case study, I have taken a random profile from my list and blurred out the sensitive details. I am going to try to understand everything there is to know about this person.

- I will start with his timelines to see what interests him.

What does it talk about?

What kind of personality do I see?

- I'll take a look at his current job…

What does he do?

How long has he been doing it?

- I will look at his pictures

Is he married?

Does he have kids?

What car does he drive?

Where does he live?

- What other content does he share that stands out from the usual. I'll keep digging inside his pictures and posts to find out more about him. I want to see, you know…

What kind of house does he have?

Is his house clean or dirty?

Does he buy trinkets?

How often does he buy expensive stuff?

Does he have expensive clothes?

What can I see inside his pictures?

Does he have pets?

Does he go to any social events?

Maybe church?

Whatever it is that I find, I'll keep writing it down.

- Once I am done with the timeline and photos, I'll make my way into the PAGE LIKES section.

The page likes are shown by recency, so you don't see what they liked five years ago when they were in high school or before they were married.

I'll take a note of all the interesting pages that they have liked inside a document.

- Then I use this chrome extension called MULTITOOLS For FACEBOOK (I am not getting into how to use this here as it's pretty simple) to pull out what kind of groups are they already a part of?

That is an incredibly powerful insight to have as not only will it tell you what kind of groups they want to join, but also where you can find communities filled with like-minded prospects.

It is also a great way of understanding what influencers they look at the most.

Not only will you know which influencers they actively engage with and gravitate towards, but you will also be able to identify the content that influencer is creating to connect with their users. They must be doing something right if your ideal client is gravitating towards them.

- As you find out more about your prospect, you should catalog and categorize all your insights.

By this point, you should have a doc filled with page likes and all the information you've gathered from their profile, page likes, groups, and influencer research.

This should include links to the top posts they are attracted to.

If you see that they like a post with a ton of engagement, chances are, that's a great post to model.

So, take that link and put it down in your doc.

- Next, I broaden the research beyond Facebook, to the entire World Wide Web.

So, let's say, your prospect is an entrepreneur. Then you want to google the best author for entrepreneurs, best book for entrepreneurs, the best podcast for entrepreneurs, top blogs for entrepreneurs, and you want to start with a very simple list.

What you want to do is model the exact way your ideal client would type into Google.

And then take notes of:

- headlines and topics,
- podcasts with high downloads,
- books with lots of reviews,
- even the chapter titles from the books,
- the review of the podcasts, courses, books, etc. will have a goldmine of information—especially the 5 star and 1-star reviews.

Remember to keep swiping whatever you find and put it inside your document.

As creepy as it may sound. When you are doing your market research, it is good to keep a picture of the prospect handy. That will allow you to tie your research to this picture, till it becomes so in tune with this person that you know EXACTLY what they think and EXACTLY what they want.

What's their worry? What are they embarrassed of? What hurts them the most?

Next, start by looking at your top competitors. **Who is your best competitor?** Go to their Facebook Page, what kind of people are engaging with their posts? Check out their advertisements. Who has given them five-star reviews? Check out their Google reviews. Go to LinkedIn and see who has talked to them. Who has mentioned them on Twitter, on Facebook?

You can find your top competitors and then you can find their top engagers and their top engagers are most probably their best fans and customers. And once you can find that, you can start researching them, and if they look like your ideal clients too, go in and repeat the process I've discussed.

Now let's see if you can use this newfound knowledge to create awesome video content.

CONSIDER ADDING A SALES VIDEO TO YOUR OFFER!

[OPTIONAL]

Whenever possible, you should consider using a VIDEO promo in your offers.

Why?

Simple… videos can bring about a massive increase in both traffic and conversions!

And you can create premium videos effortlessly with the free and easy software available today!! (never face the camera, if you don't want to!).

Steps to create videos with free software

1. <u>Use Google Slides/Keynote/Powerpoint</u> to create a slide presentation of your product description, including the benefits.
2. Use <u>Camstudio</u>, a free screen recording software, to turn your slide presentation into a video.
3. To add audio narration to your video go for a simple (good quality) microphone headset with Camstudio.

A cheap but high-quality alternative to Camstudio is <u>Camtasia / Screencast-o-Matic</u>.

Here is a stupid-simple script framework for a high-converting video:

1. First, create a personal connection by introducing yourself and stating your "USP" (more on "USP" in the next section).

2. Then build rapport by making your visitor feel comfortable by welcoming them and build trust by telling them about your above-average service/guarantee.

3. Talk about quality control.
   - If it's physical products, talk about how you inspect them before shipping, what kind of packaging you use, etc

   - If it's a software / service, talk about your round the clock support, constant improvements etc.

4. Mention your refund policy. While you do not expect to get refund requests, the fact that you're upfront about it shows that you're selling in good faith.

5. Highlight the product's greatest benefits, remembering to target your visitor's emotional 'hot spots.'

6. **Finally, give a clear 'call to action**' and thank them for trusting you as a seller. Reassure them that they won't be disappointed (and will be thrilled) and remind them that your 100% iron-clad guarantee fully and completely protects them.

Props to https://dollarshaveclub.com for this fantastic script.

Mike: 'Hi. I'm Mike – founder of DollarShave.com. What is Dollar-

Shave.com? Well, for a dollar a month we send high quality razors right to your door. Yeah. A dollar. Are the blades any good? No. Our blades are fucking great.

Mike: 'Each razor has stainless steel blades and Aloe Vera lubrication strip and a pivot head. It's so gentle a toddler could use it.'

Mike: 'And do you like spending 20 dollars a month on brand named razors – 19 go to Roger Federer – '

Mike: 'I'm good at tennis...'

Mike: 'And do you think your razor needs a vibrating handle, a flash light, a backscratcher and 10 blades? Your handsome-ass grandfather had one blade and polio.

Mike: Looking goooood poppop!

Mike: 'Stop paying for shave tech you don't need and stop forgetting to pay for your blades every month – Alejandro and I are gonna' ship them right to ya'.

Mike: 'We're not just selling razors, we're also making new jobs. Alejandro, what were you doing last month?'

Alejandro: 'Not working'

Mike: 'And what you doing now?'

Alejandro: 'Working.'

Mike: 'I'm no Vanderbulit but this train makes hay'

Mike: 'So stop forgetting to buy your blades every month and start deciding where you're gonna stack all those dollar bills [I] am saving you.'

Mike: 'We're Dollarshave.com and the party, is on.'

LEAD WITH YOUR USP

Not Your Product

The idea uncovered here will breathe new life into ANY content you create, put you on a level way above your competitors, and allow you to INSTANTLY bond with your prospects.

Furthermore, you can <u>use this epic concept not only to increase sales significantly but also to BRAND yourself as a TRUSTWORTHY and CREDIBLE expert in any niche!</u>

The concept, in a nutshell, is this: "Lead <u>with your USP (Unique Selling Position), not with your product!</u>".

Don't worry. It is easy to do.

Note: If you are not sure what we mean by "USP," you're not alone .... (see how I validated you?) **Here's the lowdown**... You can think of your USP **as your VISION**. Your VISION should tell how you plan to make your prospect's life better.

Amusingly, as you shall see, <u>we don't convey this by talking about the product, instead we convey it by talking about the prospect's life, ideally keeping it independent of the product.</u>

Here are some real life examples of brands using their USP to pack-a-punch, in all their offers!

< >

<u>McDonald's Restaurants</u> - Where most burger companies are leading with how delicious their burgers are, McDonald's commercials often lead with <u>"You deserve a break today."</u>

Notice <u>how it has no mention of their product</u> whatsoever. They are leading with their USP. Essentially McDonald's is saying,

"We know how families are always stressed out and tired. We've always felt you should have a place where you can take your family and children for a break and have fun, and spend quality time together. Oh, and by the way, also quench your hunger and thirst with a quick delicious meal that's easy on your pocket".

Oh, by the way, besides burgers, McDonald's also sells toys, action figures, glasses, and lots of other stuff you and your kids can enjoy.

By beginning with their USP, McDonald's has reached out to a far larger group of people than would have been impossible had they begun with their burgers.

With just that one opening line, they have…**"expanded their prospect pool."**

Now, even people who weren't thinking of having a burger might be enticed to check out a MacDonald's outlet to see what the excitement is all about.

<u>Disney</u> - Walt Disney started as an animator, but he had a broader vision… HE wanted to put people "inside" his movies… So he created Disneyland. Other parks followed. But Walt's TRUE vision came from him as a father. <u>He had nowhere to go with his daughter for "fun" on Sunday!</u>

Today, Disney commercials talk about family and "creating memories."

So besides movies, today, Disney has toys, clothes, theme parks, world-class golf courses, restaurants, hotels, shops, and even offer other vacation cruises.

Here's how you and I can apply this to OUR offers....

1. You can <u>deduce the product creator's "USP"</u> and lead with that OR…
2. If the product creator doesn't have a 'vision' per se (OR if you create your OWN Products), you can lead with your OWN USP.

For example, suppose as an Amazon Affiliate, we are reviewing a camcorder made by Camorama (fictitious name for illustration only). A typical "traditional' product review might go something like this…

TYPICAL PRODUCT FIRST REVIEW / PROMO - the wrong way

The Camorama 997 Camcorder X shown here comes with a unique set of very convenient features that make taking excellent videos a snap.

Here are the detailed specs… yada yada yada.

With this Camorama 997 Camcorder, you don't have to be a rocket scientist to make great, professional-looking videos.

CLICK HERE to see today's price.

By default, this would be a pretty good review/offer. It defines the product, covers the main features and benefits, and has a solid call to action telling the viewer to buy.

BUT <u>we can make it much better</u> by reversing the order and <u>leading with USP FIRST</u> and product last.

EXAMPLE 1 - "USP FIRST" PRODUCT LISTING (USING THE "COMPANY'S USP"):

With the Camorama 997 Camcorder X, Camorama PROVES it is a company that believes one does not need to be a 'rocket scientist' to make great, professional-looking videos. I am technically challenged when it comes to camcorders. I've always wondered, wouldn't it be awesome if there were a camera that blah blah... **that's why I LOVE this excellent video camera!**

(Description - specifications, features, and benefits...)

With these unique and convenient features, you'll find taking excellent videos with the Camorama 997 Camcorder X to be a snap.

CLICK HERE to see today's special price.

Note that this is precisely the SAME offer! All we've done is reversed the order and LED with the USP (that you don't need to be a rocket scientist to take great, professional-looking videos). And brought in the product LAST.

We still cover all the essential features and benefits of the camcorder, and we have a solid call to action. The difference is we END with the PRODUCT, and lead with the "USP."

We establish a personal connection with our viewer immediately and give them a strong and relatable reason to get the product even before they know anything ABOUT it.

Now let's pull the same trick with OUR USP rather than a so-called "company" USP. It's as easy as 1 2 3! We simply state the "USP" in personal terms rather than in company terms.

EXAMPLE 2 - "USP FIRST" REVIEW (YOUR OWN USP):

Making memories through videos should not be limited only to those who have the technical know-how to create a professional video. Being a technophobe myself, I have always wanted a camcorder that I can operate by myself...and now, I have one. Called Camcorder X, designed by Camorama...

(Description of features and benefits...)

With this unique set of convenient features, you'll find taking excellent videos with Camorama 997 Camcorder X to be a snap.

CLICK HERE to see today's special price.

Note that we are using the same review. All we've done is state the USP in the 1st paragraph as our own. See how, doing it like this, allows us to create a PERSONAL CONNECTION too? The fact that the camcorder is simple to operate even for a "technophobe" is reassuring for even smart users.

As you can see, leading with your vision allows you to make an instant personal connection to your visitor while simultaneously building credibility as well.

EXAMPLE 3 - WHEN THE "USP" IS NOT OBVIOUS.

SO what if the camcorder you are selling/reviewing is NOT easy to use? In that case, you need to make the complicated operation appear as a virtue. Ask yourself, **what kind of outcome would justify a complicated process?** What kind of people would prefer such a process?

YOUR "USP" might end up being something like this...

I'm tired of oversimplified "automated" video cameras that don't allow ME full and precise control of the video taking process...

There is ALWAYS a vision.

Either you need to find it, or create it based on the product and the customer "hot spot" research.

Successful politicians use 'USP' ALL THE TIME. They don't just say "I want to spend a trillion dollars we don't have to provide better education"... they say, "I believe that American's don't want to see ANY child not getting a chance because mommy and daddy can't afford to pay for school." USP FIRST.

Offer products NOT in terms of what the product features are, but rather in terms of what YOU (AND YOUR CUSTOMERS) BELIEVE

IN. Do you/they believe in...

- Keeping your/their family healthy? Safe?
- Getting products that are naturally easy to use?
- Getting the best VALUE for your/their money?
- Providing nutrition, enjoyment, and safety for your/their family?
- Indulging yourself/themselves?
- Making life fun? Etc.

<u>When promoting MULTIPLE PRODUCTS, you can also lead with a VISION.</u>

Suppose we are promoting a line of homemade jewelry on Pinterest. We could say....

"As one who wants to accessorize with jewelry, I've generally felt that one ought to have the option to look chic and stylish without breaking the bank."

Now we have positioned ourselves to sell any piece of jewelry.

If you are promoting a book on how to make money as an affiliate marketer, your vision might be, "I've always believed there had to be a way for even complete newbies to make a solid income online with affiliate marketing WITHOUT a website or a list!"

If you are promoting a book on how to get targeted traffic, your vision might be, "If you've always wanted to tell Google (with their ever-changing rules) to go screw themselves...Now You can!"

I came across a book that showed people how to use Social Media to GET traffic to their affiliate offers... the headline was **"Tell Google To Take A Hike!"**... the book was a hit and received a ton of reviews from people that said only the headline made them buy... <u>Notice the headline doesn't even tell what the product is!!</u>

Now in the copy, the product was fully revealed and described, but consider this... If the headline had led with something like

"Make money with Social Media" or some such, many people would say, "Oh, I'm not interested in social media… sounds like a lot of work… **And stopped reading.**

But being able to tell Google to take a hike?? Now people are saying, "I don't care what I have to do… I WANT THIS POWER!!!"

USP FIRST.

SECTION II – SECRETS TO CREATING POWERFULLY PERSUASIVE SALES COPY

That Will Earn You MORE Money with LESS Traffic

If you continuously run into a wall trying to write persuasive 'copy' for your offers, you are not alone (see how I VALIDATED you?)... Most people cannot write good copy that converts well.

<u>With the stupid-simple ideas outlined below, you will be writing highly persuasive copy in no time!</u>

This section is geared to beginners and advanced marketers alike. Everything is broken down into bite-sized easy to understand segments that will have you creating a powerfully persuasive copy in no time! (for ANY promotion!).

You will learn....

- How to craft POLARIZING headlines that practically force people to read your offer (more straightforward than you think!).

- How to repeatedly hit those all-important emotional hot-spots that leave people wanting to click BUY.

NOW!

- **An underused way to get your reader to abandon any skepticism** and blindly accept everything you say!

- A simple trick that can even **get "skim readers" to SLOW DOWN** and read everything!

- **How to increase "perceived value,"** so you can charge higher prices and get more conversions!

- **How to add "Power words" and Descriptors** to maximize sales!

- How can you **state your Guarantee** in a way that makes it seem MUCH MORE VALUABLE (and **virtually eliminates refunds!**)

...and much more! You'll also learn....

1. How to Easily Create Powerful Headlines That Boost Your Conversions Up To 500%.

2. Special considerations for Email promos, Social Media Promos, Amazon Book Promos! - If you promote through email, social media, or self-publish Amazon Books (or plan to), this module will be a godsend worth more to you than the rest of the book!

PIYUSH AGARWAL

Here we go!

THE ONE SUPER-EXPLOSIVE TECHNIQUE THAT YOU CAN USE TO BLOW UP YOUR CONVERSIONS

Features vs. Benefits

To write compelling sales copy that truly persuades people to buy, we need to familiarize ourselves with the concept of product "features" and product "benefits". Your offers need to contain BOTH hand in hand, but BENEFITS are the more important and influential of the two.

The BIGGEST mistake I see beginner (and veteran!!!) copywriters making is they <u>fail to flood their sales copy with powerful emotion triggering BENEFITS</u>.

ANY sales copy or promotion can be improved by ADDING MORE BENEFITS!

Features are great, but BENEFITS SELL...

<u>So what is the difference between a "feature" and a "benefit"?</u>

Simply put, a "feature" is an aspect of the product... It is the "what," for example, a cordless drill "feature" might be that it has a "variable speed drill."

A "benefit" on the other hand is the advantage or WHY the feature is useful, "variable speed drill" allows you the BENEFIT of being able to control the hole position and depth much more quickly and drill much more precisely.

See how this ties in with what we discussed earlier about triggering an emotional response in the viewer?

A feature can trigger a puzzled, questioning, or defensive response. In other words, the reader may ask why they are being told that the drill is variable speed.

On the other hand, when you reveal to the reader that a variable speed drill will enable them to control the hole position and depth better, you can **almost certainly trigger a positive emotional response in them.**

When possible, attach EMOTION to your benefits too! "No more headaches, frustration, or embarrassing mistakes."

For an example of a 'feature' vs. a 'benefit,' look at the title/subtitle to this guide.

**Discover The Insider Secrets To
Creating Hypnotic Offers For ANYTHING!**

**Generate YOUR OWN Army of Hungry Loyal Customers (for ANY Product!)
And Explode Your Profits by 300% or More!**

The title is the FEATURE... It tells you WHAT this book is - Namely, it will show you how to create hypnotic offers...

Within the subtitle are BENEFITS... Clearly defining WHY the feature is good - <u>it will Generate YOUR OWN ARMY of Hungry</u>

Loyal Buyers (For ANY PRODUCT!) And Explode Your Profits by 300% or MORE!

You will definitely list product features in the promotion, but you must also remember to couple those features with BENEFITS, BENEFITS and MORE BENEFITS.

The perceived value of the product(s) is directly proportional to the number of benefits you state in your offer. The more benefits you enlist, the higher the perceived value is.

The question is, how do you best present these 'BENEFITS' for the prospect?

Truly knowing your prospects' "hotspots" will give you a significant edge in benefit-hunting, which we discussed in section I.

Again. ALWAYS remember that people buy on EMOTION. So, as said, where possible, <u>your benefits should be packaged with emotion!</u>

Remember our 'camera' example in section I, where we turned "red-eye" into "embarrassing red-eye"? Let's expand on that…

"In any photo, "red-eye" immediately brands you as an amateurish photographer. People will soon be too embarrassed to be photographed by you (after all, who wants to look like the devil??!?) This camera automatically prevents the <u>embarrassment</u> of red eyes showing up in your photos. Your friends will MARVEL at how you always seem to take perfect pictures!"

Here are some other examples…

The fish depth finder doesn't just locate where there's plenty of fish (the feature); it catches you the BIGGEST FISH making you the envy of every other fisher! (the emotion loaded BENEFIT).

That book doesn't just show you how to make money doing online marketing (the feature), it provides you more leisure time/ family time, eliminates stress, brings vacations, earns you the admiration of friends, freedom from a 9-5 grind, the ability to fire your boss, the pride of owning your own successful business, etc. (the emotion loaded BENEFITS).

Bear in mind that despite using logic to "rationalize" their purchases, people ALWAYS buy on emotion!

Put another way, always remember, "What's in it for me?" (WIIFM) That is the question your prospect will always ask! ANSWER that question with benefits, benefits, and benefits.

- Add EMOTION to your benefits.
- Add exciting adjectives too!
- Validate your prospect.
- Hit those emotional triggers!

HOW TO BUILD PERCEIVED VALUE WITH IMAGES AND ILLUSTRATION

They say an image is worth a thousand words, but with sales copy, images are worth a thousand dollars! Human beings are visual by nature. Images trigger our emotions, and, as said, it's the emotion that triggers buying.

Nice images break up dull print, excite the reader, and create a very professional look too. Even basic videos made out of Power-Point presentations are brought to life with strategic images.

Images can be of...
- the product itself,
- or the product being used,
- or they can be illustrations classifying the "parts" of the product or classifying different FEATURES of the product.
- Images can also show the product from different angles and confirm the product being "used" in different ways or different settings.

You can take your photos or get images by using Google's advanced image search.

IMPORTANT: Within the Google Advanced Image search tool, scroll down to where it says "usage right" and use the drop-down menu to select **"free to use, share, or modify, even commercially."**

You can also use photos to reinforce what the print is saying. If your BENEFIT is that your product or book will show the prospect how to earn money in their spare time, and <u>you have a picture of a bright-eyed, smiling person excitedly waving a wad of cash in the air,</u> you are reinforcing your print with an image!

A famous news reporter once confessed just how powerful "images" can be... He was talking of photos of meetings between heads of state... He said if the pictures (and video) all show the two leaders smiling, laughing, and shaking hands, and he says, "My sources say the meeting went very poorly," he will NOT be believed!! The smiling faces contradict the narrative, and when this happens, people reject the story and go with the image!

Go through your copy and ask yourself, "What image(s) might I insert to reinforce and back up my words?"...

Here are some examples of images backing up the sales copy words...

See how the image of an excited 3-year old girl (a very specific age) is a big asset for the ad. It instantly conveys fun and entertainment and is going to grab the parents' attention with kids this age.

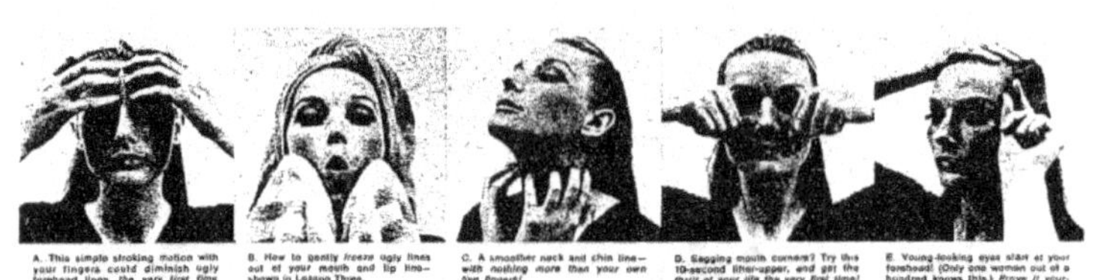

Also, notice the second ad by Gene Schwartz that targets middle-aged women trying to lose wrinkles. The image of 5 women using different massaging techniques to remove wrinkles builds enough curiosity to grab attention and compel the reader to check out the ad.

WITHOUT THIS, YOUR SALES WILL PLUMMET

Always, always, ALWAYS and ALWAYS include multiple 'calls to action' in your offers! Don't assume people will click buy, or "know" what to do - TELL THEM WHAT TO DO!!. The ONLY WAY you make money is when your visitor clicks the BUY NOW Button (or subscribe button), so you're leaving money on the table if you don't guide visitors right up to the all-important BUY NOW.

Multiple 'calls to action' usually work best with a 'soft/subtle' call to action early in the offer, with stronger 'calls to action' toward the end of the text.

Examples of "soft" calls to action might be...
- Check out the independent reviews here.
- Get more info here.
- Click here to see if this is for you.

Examples of "strong" calls to action might be...
- Get your copy now before this price goes up.
- Get your copy now before the offer closes forever.
- Get your copy now before I decide to pull my bonus.

Another tip is to contrast the benefit of clicking vs the consequence of not clicking on the Button. For example…

"Click now and get free shipping" (benefit), "limited stock - Once it's gone, it's gone." (consequence).

"Click now to buy at a discounted price" (benefit), "don't be hating yourself later for missing out" (consequence).

"Click now and never have to worry about getting traffic again!" (benefit) "or pass and continue to fail with what doesn't work" (consequence),

"Yes, I want to grow my email list 4x" **(benefit)** vs "No thanks, I'll make do with a small list" **(consequence)**.

HOW TO CREATE POWERFUL HEADLINES / TITLES THAT VIRTUALLY FORCE YOUR PROSPECTS TO READ YOUR COMPLETE OFFER!

In any promotion, lots of headlines are good CRUCIAL. You will always have a main headline and use the additional headlines as subs within the promo body.

There are two reasons why you want to do this…

1. Subheadlines (within the body of the promo) create "white space," breaking up long text into bite-sized pieces encouraging the visitor to read your complete

offer.

2. Catchy subheads can also serve to keep your viewer engaged in your promo. Subtitles can also slow down "skim readers" and cause them to stop and read the body of the description more slowly.

For example, what looks and reads better?...

Burberry Ultimate Edition

Yada yada yada yad yada yada yada yada. Yada yada yada yad yada yada yada yada. Yada yada yada yad yada yada yada yada. Yada yada yada yad yada yada yada yada. Yada yada yada yad yada yada yada yada. Yada yada yada yad

Yada yada yada yad yada yada yada yada. Yada yada yada yad yada yada yada yada. Yada yada yada yad yada yada yada yada. Yada yada yada yad yada yada yada yada. Yada yada yada yada. Yada yada yada yad yada yada yada yada. Yada yada yada yad yada yada yada.

Yada yada yada yad yada yada yada yada. Yada yada yada yad yada yada yada yada. Yada yada yada yad yada yada yada yada. Yada yada yada yad yada yada yada yada. Yada yada yada yad yada yada yada yada. Yada yada yada yad yada yada yada yada. Yada yada yada yad yada yada yada yada. Yada yada yada yad yada yada yada yada. Yada yada yada yad yada yada yada yada. Yada yada yada yad yada yada yada yada. Yada yada yada yada. Yada yada yada yad yada yada yada yada.

Yada yada yada yad yada yada yada yada. Yada yada yada yad yada yada yada yada. Yada yada yada yad yada yada yada yada. Yada yada yada yad yada yada yada yada. Yada yada yada yada. Yada yada yada yad yada yada yada yada.

---x---x---

Or....

Latest Spring - Summer Collection!
Burberry Limited Edition Up To 30% OFF
3 Day Flash Sale!

Get The Best Value For Your Dollar

Yada yada yada yad yada yada yada yada. Yada yada yada yad yada yada yada yada. Yada yada yada yad yada yada yada yada. Yada yada yada yad yada yada yada yada. Yada yada yada yad yada yada yada yada.

Get Great Fashion + Extended Warranty Too.

Yada yada yada yad yada yada yada yada. Yada yada yada yad yada yada yada yada. Yada yada yada yad yada yada yada yada. Yada yada yada yad yada yada yada yada. Yada yada yada yad yada yada yada yada. Yada yada yada yad yada yada yada yada.

Get A Sign of True Success In Your Wrist

Yada yada yada yad yada yada yada yada. Yada yada yada yad yada yada yada yada. Yada yada yada yad yada yada yada yada. Yada yada yada yad yada yada yada yada. Yada yada yada yad yada yada yada yada.

The Real Burberry Watches! Not Cheap Knock-Offs

Yada yada yada yad yada yada yada yada. Yada yada yada yad yada yada yada yada. Yada yada yada yad yada yada yada yada. Yada yada yada yad yada yada yada yada. Yada yada yada yad yada yada yada yada.

---x---x---

In the 2nd example, we see how subheadlines make the text much more scannable for the reader, the extra white space added gives room to breathe and makes it less daunting (also don't forget to mix in some photos).

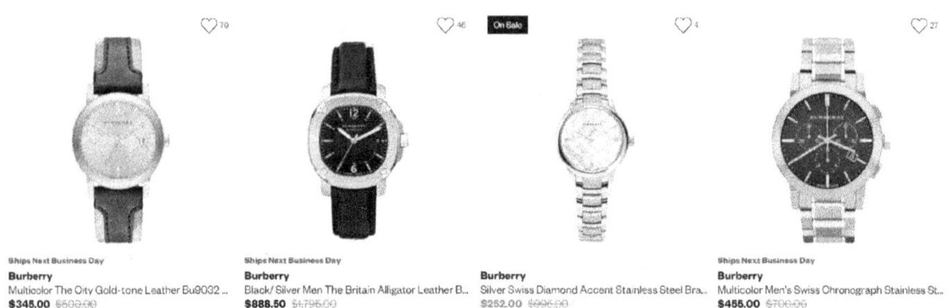

In the example above, we also see how <u>adding a pre-headline and sub-headline to the main headline</u> helps attract attention and build more value while inviting the reader to read on.

Even though your offer has a title, there's nothing wrong with inserting a pre-headline/main headline/subheadline at the top of your product description review, or promo.

A super-simple way for remembering the difference between pre-headlines, primary headline, and subheadings is to remember that, in most cases, the primary HEADLINE contains the major or leading benefit of the product offered.

Spend as long on the headline as you do on the rest of the offer. <u>It is the headline that draws the reader to read your offer.</u>

Write as many benefit-driven headlines as possible and then pick out or combine the best ones to form your main headline. Use the remaining headlines as additional sub-titles within your copy. (to pile on additional product benefits).

There are many types of headlines that have been used over the years, but the two BEST and SIMPLEST are the "Curiosity Arousing" Headline, or the "Main Benefit" headline.

You can also use a headline / sub-headline to convey a "main feature," followed by a "main benefit."

Meanwhile, the additional subtitles within the promo body act as "periodic attention grabbers" that re-activate the reader's urge, keep them engaged, and draw them (repeatedly) into the text!

In any event, always make sure that your headlines trigger EMOTION!

It's also good to <u>use a HOOK</u> in your main title (all titles, if possible!). In the case of the above title, it was a UPTO 30% OFF DISCOUNT. We could use one of the following title hooks!

- **Burberry Watches New Collection - Free Shipping**
- **Burberry Watches New Collection - Avoid Counterfeit Ripoffs**
- **Burberry Watches New Collection + Early Bird DISCOUNT!**

Etc..

On the other hand, just as the main headline draws the reader into the text, the pre-headline should draw the reader in the main headline.

One of my favorite pre-headline styles is the "Warning" type.
- WARNING: Don't Buy Another _________ Until You See This.
- WARNING: Don't Be Fooled By Imitations.
- WARNING: What Your Vet Isn't Telling You.
- Don't Fall Prey To Other Offers of Inferior Quality.

Here's another headline tip. **The more SPECIFIC the headline, the better.** For example, look at the following "headlines."

"How To Make Money"
"How To Make Money Online"
"How To Make $300 A Day Online."
"How To Make $347.32 A Day on Amazon Listing Items You Can Find For A Quarter."

The last line is pretty specific.

It has the highest chance of getting read because the title clearly tells the reader <u>what they are going to get and what the benefit to them is</u>!

Always go for the specific titles/headlines over the general ones. Consider...

- RayBan Sunglasses
- RayBan Sunglasses GasCan
- RayBan Sunglasses GasCan Black/Ice Iridium Polarized 60 mm Lens
- RayBan Sunglasses GasCan Black/Ice Iridium Polarized 60 mm Lens - Free Shipping.

The last title clearly tells the reader exactly what they are going to get and adds a benefit (free shipping).

Also, chances are the last title will be found by many more people because it contains many more search terms that people will be searching for.

REMEMBER that every headline must invoke a strong emotion AND communicate a huge BENEFIT!

For example, I might take our two highly specific headlines from above and add some EMOTIONALLY CHARGED benefit...

"How To Make $247.32 A Day on Amazon Selling Items You Can Find For a Quarter And Gain The Financial Freedom You and Your Family Deserve".

"RayBan Sunglasses GasCan Black/Ice Iridium Polarized 60mm Lens - Free Shipping, Remove Dangerous Glare While Driving And Look Cool Doing it!"

So, in summary, your headlines need to...
- Be specific
- Convey A Strong Benefit
- Trigger EMOTION

- Draw the reader into the crux of your copy
- Where possible, VALIDATE your prospect and echo their beliefs…

The above are examples of BENEFITS driven headlines. Here is an example of a "curiosity producing" headline…

The product was how to create a Sudoku Puzzle Book for Profit. The book showed how to create the puzzles using FREE software, create the books with ZERO money invested, and get the books automatically shown for sale on hundreds of bookstore sites, including Amazon, Barnes and Noble, and more…

The headline of the promo went something like this…

How Would You Like To Sell A Unique (LEGAL) Product on Autopilot That's More Addictive Than Cocaine!!? (And FREE To Create)

It's brilliant. Why??!?, because there was a peculiar incident that happened during that time in an <u>Australian drug-related trial, where 5 of the 12 Jurors were caught doing Sudoku instead of listening to evidence!!!</u>

And to top it off, the sub-headline stated…

… Free Bonus - How to Create Maze Puzzle Books

That headline certainly triggered my emotions!… a Unique LEGAL product more addictive than cocaine? … sold on autopilot? … FREE to create?? WOW! How could you not check out that promotion to see what it was about?

The headline conveys a strong benefit, is specific, and creates a specific emotional picture or VISION. It certainly draws the reader into your copy.

The copy went on to relate the court case story… It says, "the jurors weren't caught snorting cocaine, they were not caught smoking marijuana, they were not caught drinking alcohol or even smoking cigarettes, but they were caught doing Sudoku puzzles!"

The creator did a great job with the copy, but he also did a fantastic job with the images.

Here are 2 more examples of headlines that NAILED it (and used graphics/images to reinforce the message)...

If you are lucky enough to have any money set aside for a rainy day and you're keeping it in a savings account, you are really being taken.

Your money is probably earning about 5¾ per cent interest. Since inflation is averaging 8 per cent to 10 per cent a year, you are not even breaking even. And the way things are going this year it can only get worse.

Do you realize that you have to spend $1.49 to buy as much steak as you could buy for a dollar only a few months ago?

If you have any money invested in the stock market, you are really asking for it. Eighteen months ago Winnebago was considered one of the safest of the blue chip stocks on the New York Stock Exchange. A thousand dollars invested in this "safe" stock only a year and a half ago, as of this writing, would have shrunk to $145.00. And hundreds of stocks have done even worse.

What about U.S. Savings Bonds? As an investment they are really a joke. Ten years ago if you had invested $1,000.00 of your hard earned money in series "E" government bonds you would have by now earned only $7.44 a year in purchasing power.

Well, how about keeping your money hidden in an old sock under the mattress? Had you tucked away a thousand dollars in this manner in 1957, by now your purchasing power would have dropped a full 40 per cent. Are things about to get better?

No way.

The year 1974 promises to produce the highest inflation rate in the last 22 years. Prices, as you may have noticed, are going no where but up. Some, like meat and gasoline are going right out of sight. The plain fact is that your money is in more danger right now than at anytime since 1929.

Is there a way out? Is there any place at all to put your money where it is safe? Where will it earn enough interest to keep ahead of inflation? Where you can get at it instantly in case of an emergency? Is there?

You bet there is!

The answer is going to surprise you. The best place to keep your money is probably the same place you are keeping it now. In your bank in a savings account. You've got to start doing things a little differently, however.

Here is just one of the things you can do if you know how. You can go to your bank, take out your savings, fill out a new deposit ticket, put the money right back into another savings account and increase the interest on your savings from 6 to 15 per cent. All in one day! Hard to believe isn't it? But this is just the beginning.

Listen to all of this!

- *When you open a new account you can get ten bank gifts instead of one.*
- *You can withdraw your money and still earn interest on it.*
- *You can have two savings accounts paying you interest at the same time on the same money.*
- *You can earn interest on money you have spent months ago.*
- *You can earn more money on your checking account than most people earn on their savings accounts.*
- *You can earn interest on the money other people have on deposit.*

All of this is perfectly legal. Everything you will be doing is not only permitted but actually encouraged by banks and other financial institutions because the more money you make the more money they make. In fact, they use these techniques themselves. And during all this, your money will be insured 100 per cent by the U.S. Government. All of this is carefully explained in a new book titled, "How to Rob a Bank Without a Gun."

The book was written by an Ohio school teacher named George Jenney as part of a research project for a publishing company. The book is easy-to-read, easy-to-understand, and can lead you step-by-step to a new financial independence. The book is not now available at book stores or newsstands.

You can get a copy if you hurry by sending your name and address and $6.95 in cash, check, or money order payable to The Good News Publishing Co., Dept. No. 1178, 7576 Freedom Ave., N.W., North Canton, Ohio 44720.

The book will be sent to you promptly by return mail. The publisher guarantees that this book will show you how to at least double the earning power of your money.

If not, or for any reason you are dissatisfied, you can return the book for a full and immediate refund of your entire purchase price. You can't lose.

Send for the book today. Remember, now more than ever you have a real money fight on your hands and it is only going to get worse.

Here is a chance to put the odds on your side.

A masterpiece by the great Gary Halbert. The headline… <u>"How to keep your money from being MURDERED,"</u> and the image of a 'knife cutting through a pile of cash'… is a powerful combination. It builds so much curiosity…. How can you murder money?... why…. Is my money being murdered?.... How can I prevent it? **Even if you cannot murder money, the very thought of murdering money raises curiosity and fear.**

Now take a look at another interesting example from the same writer…

PIYUSH AGARWAL

New York Times; Mar 3, 1974; pg. 433

HOW TO MAKE MONEY WITH YOUR CREDIT CARDS

You may have more money in your pocket than you realize. A lot more. In fact, chances are that you have virtually thousands of dollars of "hidden money" in your wallet or purse right now.

Before you can spend this money you are going to have to do a little work. It will take you about 45 minutes. That is approximately how long it will take you to learn 31 legal ways to turn every credit card you have from an expense into a plastic gold mine.

This isn't exactly what the Credit Card Companies had in mind when they issued you your card. But please don't spend a lot of time feeling sorry for them. They have been making money from you from the first day you ever used any of your credit cards. Not only have they been making money from you, they have also been taking a healthy cut from the restaurants, stores, hotels, and other places where you use your cards. Credit card company profits over the years have amounted to millions, upon millions, upon millions of dollars.

So don't start feeling guilty just because you are about to learn how to use your credit cards to make yourself a few thousand extra dollars. Actually, you aren't going to be hurting the credit card companies anyway.

Just in case you are wondering, each of these money-making techniques is perfectly safe. They are also 100 per cent legal and they will not in any way endanger your credit or your standing with the Credit Card Companies. They are the result of a great deal of painstaking research. The results of this research have been nothing short of amazing. Here are some of the things you can do with your credit cards if you know how:

- You can earn interest (up to 7½ per cent) on money you have already spent.
- If you can memorize two short sentences you can flash your credit card and get sizeable discounts on even the things you pay cash for.
- You can use your credit cards to raise thousands of dollars in cash even if banks and finance companies refuse to give you a loan. And you can do this without anyone approving your credit or making a credit investigation.
- You can cut the interest rate you are paying on your credit card purchases by as much as 50 per cent.

- You can use your credit cards to keep your money at the same time you are spending it and earn interest on it all at the same time.
- You can use credit card company money for as long as 90 days without paying any interest at all.
- You can get up to 40 different credit cards and use each one of them for your own personal profit.

You can use your credit cards to do all this legally and safely. It's amazing but true! But here is something even more amazing. When you use these smart-money techniques you will actually be doing a favor for everyone involved including the Credit Card Companies themselves.

All of this is carefully explained in a brand new book titled, *"How To Turn Plastic Into Gold."* The book was written by Martin J. Meyer, one of the nation's foremost experts on making money and saving money for you—when you bank—when you buy—when you use your credit card. The book is easy to read, easy to understand, and inexpensive. You can get a copy if you hurry by sending your name and address and $6.95 in cash, check or money order payable to The Good News Publishing Co., 7576 Freedom Ave., N.W., Dept. 1087 , North Canton, Ohio 44720. The book will be sent to you promptly by return mail.

If for any reason you should be dissatisfied, you can return the book and your $6.95 will be immediately refunded.

See how the Headline and the Image play together to get the reader gripped and eager to find out more. **MASSIVE MASSIVE CURIOSITY IN ACTION.** The headline - "How To Make Money With Credit Cards" and a picture of a "Man sitting on a huge pile of money with credit cards in his hand smiling" gives so much context and reassurance on the claim made with the headline.

As you read further, the introductory paragraph successfully paints a "buying environment" and builds context for the conversation by making the reader even more curious.

And then goes on to set up a common enemy for the author and the reader, the "credit card companies."

The writer is swift to make the reader curious, invite him into the copy, set the environment, establish a common ground, and identify a common enemy.

To construct a headline, I usually start by listing every possible benefit of the product and determining which is the strongest benefit. Are there benefits that I am yet to think of? What emotions can I trigger?

Then I'll start writing simple headlines and then adding descriptors and emotional triggers. I usually end up taking pieces of headlines and rearranging them and mixing them until I come up with something dynamite…. Then I keep looking for something better…

Remember that you DON'T want to "overhype" but you DO want to evoke emotion.

If your headline says, "How To Make A Million A Year Blogging," few will believe that (even if it's true)… On the other hand, say "How Anyone Can Make $2,247.00 A Month Blogging PART TIME, Using FREE Software", and you'll have offered the reader a tantalizing prospect few will want to miss out on.

Keep a swipe file of headlines you can adapt for your uses (refer to the next section for more on 'swiping'). You can often adapt headlines (or parts of headlines) from entirely different niches to your niche. **Magazine covers** can be excellent sources for swiping headline ideas too!

Finally, **use an easy to read font for your headlines**. Use a color that stands out but is easy on the eyes. Make sure your font color contrasts with the background for easy readability. For example, I've used black, red, or blue text on a white or very light grey background, so the print stands out without blinding the reader (stay away from neon or glowing colors).

> **Alternatively, A White Text on A Black Background Can Work Too (again Contrast And Easy On The Eyes)**

HOW TO GET THE GREATEST COPYWRITERS TO WRITE YOUR COPY FOR FREE!

Referring back to the previous section, a swipe file doesn't just apply to headlines. It can be a file of good lines to use ANYWHERE in the sales copy. What this means is you DON'T EVER have to start copywriting from scratch! You have a whole ARMY of professional copywriters who have already written tons of amazing stuff for you!

- When you come across other people's (successful) offers or even across other product sales pages, swipe parts of the copy that grab your attention or inspire excitement in you or cause you to crave that product.

- When you come across a particularly good sales letter, make a note of, and save the parts that "excited" you!

- Before you list on eBay or Amazon, look for other successful listings in your niche and swipe their best lines.

- I often watch infomercials! (Not to shop, but to pick up clever sales pitches and exciting marketing phrases I can later adopt!)

Start by keeping a swipe file of headlines. As said, often, a headline in a completely different niche can be adapted to your niche.

Keep a swipe of power words and phrases that trigger emotions (reference my power words bonus at the end).

Keep a swipe file of phrases too (also at the end).

And, as said, keep a swipe file of entire sales letters too!

I use the Evernote Chrome extension and android app to maintain my swipe file.

Famed copywriter **John Caples** penned an ad in 1926 with the now-famous headline, "They laughed when I Sat Down At The Piano But When I Started To Play!" - Indeed, an emotion triggering headline!

I remember reading about that headline when I was studying copywriting techniques a few years back.

Recently I heard a radio commercial. The voice said...At the French Restaurant, she lauded at me when I said I could order in French, but when I said to the waiter, Nous aimerions Votre filet mignon cuit à point Avec Votre Meilleur vin rouge maison....

This 21st-century modern radio commercial was swiping a headline that's almost 100 years old!

ALWAYS KEEP A SWIPE FILE!

FYI: For the sales copy of this book, I searched through the sales copy for other copywriting books... I swiped, adapted, and rewrote parts of what others had written and added it to what I had come up with on my own…

As a BONUS, looking at my competitor's sales copy helped me define my USP!… I ASKED, <u>How can I make MY book better than the rest?</u> How can I make it stand out? (ANSWER - I don't just talk about copywriting, but I also go into "buying psychology" and cover how to <u>emotionally connect with your readers so they will buy even with mediocre sales copy)</u>.

A NEAT TRICK THAT WILL MAKE YOUR SALES COPY SING!

If you make your own products, something that works well for producing a very persuasive copy is to write your sales page before you create your product! Free from the limitations of a "real" product, you can then create a sales page that describes your ultimate "dream" product.

Once the copy is ready, go and create a product that lives up to its copy!

The result is both a better copy AND an even better end product!

This can also apply to BONUSES that you create! Let's say you are thinking of creating a BONUS PDF for an info-product. You can create your description of the bonus BEFORE you create the PDF. Chances are you'll end up with a badass bonus that is way better than your original idea!

When you write your product or bonus, you may think of yet more benefits you can add to your copy.

ALSO, the hardest part about creating a product is often writing that opening paragraph or chapter... With the copywriting predone, you already know how to start your product or bonus… "Welcome, this report will show you [ref your copy].....done!"

In other words, by writing your copy FIRST, your product creation and copy creation become a symbiotic and synergistic process where the whole is greater than the sum.

A STUPID-SIMPLE WAY TO BUILD TREMENDOUS PERCEIVED VALUE IN ALL YOUR OFFERS!

Remember that everything in your copy is aimed at creating (and increasing) "perceived value" for your product. Features with lots of enticing benefits increase perceived value.

Testimonials increase perceived value.

A strong guarantee increases perceived value.

And so on.

One of the most potent ways to increase perceived value is to stop comparing "apples to apples" and start comparing "apples to oranges"!

What do we mean by this? Simple... Suppose your product is a self-help eBook. Instead of comparing it to other similar eBooks in your niche and showing why yours is better (comparing apples to apples), compare it to seminars in the niche that people paid hundreds or even thousands of dollars for (comparing apples to oranges).

What has more "value" in your mind? A book that is better than another $49 book? Or a book that teaches you everything covered in a $3,500.00 seminar? Get the idea?

Other ways of comparing "apples to oranges" can include citing the number of years "experience" it took you to "learn" everything revealed in the book (which your readers can now gain in a few hours of study), OR the copy could cite that to learn what's in the $49 book, the author had to spend over $10,427 in other products or spend 5,297 hours finding the resources revealed in the book, etc.

If you are promoting a tool, a piece of software, or even a kitchen appliance, instead of comparing it to similar competing brands (apples to apples), compare it to the TIME and MONEY it will save the user! (apples to oranges).

For example, you could say, "With this cover creation software, I can create stunning and professional looking ecovers in minutes instead of hours! I have SAVED OVER THREE HUNDRED DOLLARS (and counting) not having to outsource this!" (apples to oranges).

Instead of saying, "this home food processor slices faster than other home food processors" (apples to apples) you can say, "With this new food processor, I'm slicing and dicing faster than a sous chef, and my meals look & taste better than the ones served by 5-star restaurants!" (apples to oranges).

If you promote collectibles, instead of citing the rarity of the collectible (or in addition to citing this), you can mention the even more rare "source" of the collectibles and tell a story about how hard it was for you to find these.

If you are promoting art, you could say something like, "100 years ago, only the very rich had beautiful art pieces hanging from their mansion walls - But today, virtually everyone can enjoy the beauty and warmth of great art pieces placed in every room of their home" (apples to oranges).

Another place where you should be comparing apples to oranges is in the price of the product. "For the price of less than a dinner for two at McDonald's plus a movie, you can enjoy this wonderful product for years!" (apples to oranges).

"This home workout training costs just a fraction of what a gym membership would cost, and it will give you better quicker results to boot!" (apples to oranges).

One of the best 'Apples to Oranges' promos I saw was a FB ad that asked, "What would you rather have? A thriving business? Or a cup of coffee?"... (the implication being the product being offered was cheaper than the cost of a starbucks coffee!)

TURN YOUR GUARANTEE INTO A VALUABLE BENEFIT!

In any promo, you ALWAYS ALWAYS want to have a guarantee, and you want to make it a powerful one. State it explicitly. The number of sales you LOSE by having a weak or non-existent guarantee will virtually ALWAYS exceed the few refunds you'll get by having a stronger guarantee!

The guarantee is a FEATURE. How it **reduces the buyer's risk** is the BENEFIT. Always remember to stress the BENEFIT.

Instead of saying, "I have a 60-day guarantee," say something like this…

'I am so confident you will be thrilled with this product, that I'm going to do something extraordinary for you - I'm going to remove all risk from you and put it all on ME and ME ALONE! I'm going to give you this Iron-Clad "No Questions Asked" Full Protection Guarantee.' (notice how the descriptor words add POWER to the Guarantee? Notice how SPECIAL we are making the customer feel?).

Take a FULL ~~30 days~~ **60 Days** to look over and enjoy this product. If you are not absolutely thrilled with your purchase for any reason, I will happily refund you in full (including shipping!), so you're not out one single penny! - I am that confident you will love this.

See how we turn a simple guarantee into something of VALUE? Whatever your guarantee, remember to state in terms that BUILD VALUE.

Remember, what matters is not WHAT you give in your guarantee, but HOW YOUR CUSTOMERS FEEL when you give it!

As an example, let's take the guarantee we saw above, and tweak it.

"My refund policy is crystal clear: I take all the risk. You have a FULL 90-days to review this product. If you are not satisfied for any reason and utterly thrilled with the exciting info contained within this book, you get a FULL 100% no questions asked refund.

No amount of money is more than your happiness for me. So, I'm more than happy to honor my words. I'm that confident you'll love this product.

See how I turn the Guarantee into an endorsement for the book?

Another way you could state it is, "Now if this book were any less than excellent, and I wasn't fully confident you will succeed with it, would I make a guarantee like that?"

Stating your Guarantee is YOUR chance to reassure your customer, make them feel special, AND even sneak in an endorsement for your product

HOW TO LIGHT A FIRE UNDER THE BUYERS' BUTT, SO THEY BUY NOW!

Ever wonder why "dime sales" are so famous (in a "dime sale" the product price continuously climbs every so many sales)? It's because it creates "urgency"!

Your copy needs to light a fire under the butts of your viewers, so they buy NOW! (not later). We do this by creating <u>scarcity</u> and <u>urgency</u>.

Examples of creating "scarcity" can include…
Limited Edition - Only 100 Will Be Sold! Once they are gone, they are gone.
Get yours today while they are in stock - I'm not sure we can ever get more!
Collector Item - stock very limited! Etc.

Examples of creating "urgency" can include…
Price goes up in 3 days.
Early bird special bonus for the first 100 buyers only.
Get this before your competition does! Etc.

HOW TO DRAW YOUR READER INTO YOUR COPY?

In any 'copy,' you want to (need to!) draw your reader in. As said previously, The pre-headline draws your viewer into the main and sub-headlines. And those headlines, in turn, draw the viewer into your 1st paragraph. That 1st (opening) paragraph is critical. It must pull your reader into the rest of your sales copy!

Granted, if your headline sucks, nothing will get read...BUT Assuming you have a great headline, your promo will still fail if you don't have a powerful opening paragraph.

Your main headline must contain your most potent benefit. Your **1st paragraph** must cover a **strong benefit** too (usually expanding on and reinforcing the benefit stated in your main headline). Its purpose is to **hit on the main emotional trigger** of your viewer and draw them into reading your offer further.

This 1st paragraph is also where you need to deepen your connection to your viewer and provide your vision. As you can guess, it's a good idea for you to spend a good amount of time on your opening paragraph.

A general rule of the thumb is you should spend as much time on your opening paragraph as you do on the entire rest of your description body, and you should spend as long on your main headline as you do on your opening paragraph and rest of the text body <u>combined</u>.

Tip: While writing your headlines, if you find some of them becoming too long, you can develop them into your opening paragraphs. #efficiency.

To write an opening paragraph, you want to talk as you would talk <u>in-person to a friend</u>. Write as if you are <u>talking to an individual</u>, <u>not a large crowd of readers</u>. Write out the most enticing and most significant benefit in emotional terms and then go back and add-in descriptor power words. Don't overhype… Keep it honest and straightforward… but still exciting!

Think of your opening paragraph as a bridge between the headline and the rest of the copy. If you can't <u>sustain the excitement</u> created by the headline by the opening paragraph, there's a very good chance that the viewer will not read the rest of your offer.

It's your chance to build trust, credibility, and likeability. The rest of your sales copy may reveal tons of additional benefits for your reader, but they won't read all that if your opening paragraph is weak.

A Simple Trick If You Suck At Writing

Writing opening paragraphs can be a challenge when you first attempt them (swipe files help!). Here's a simple way to get around the difficulty: Make the opening paragraph a brief sentence or two, followed by a series of bullet points.

Bullet points are great because they are easy to read, create white space, and are great for skim readers too!

Here's a modern example of an opening paragraph that uses bullet points….

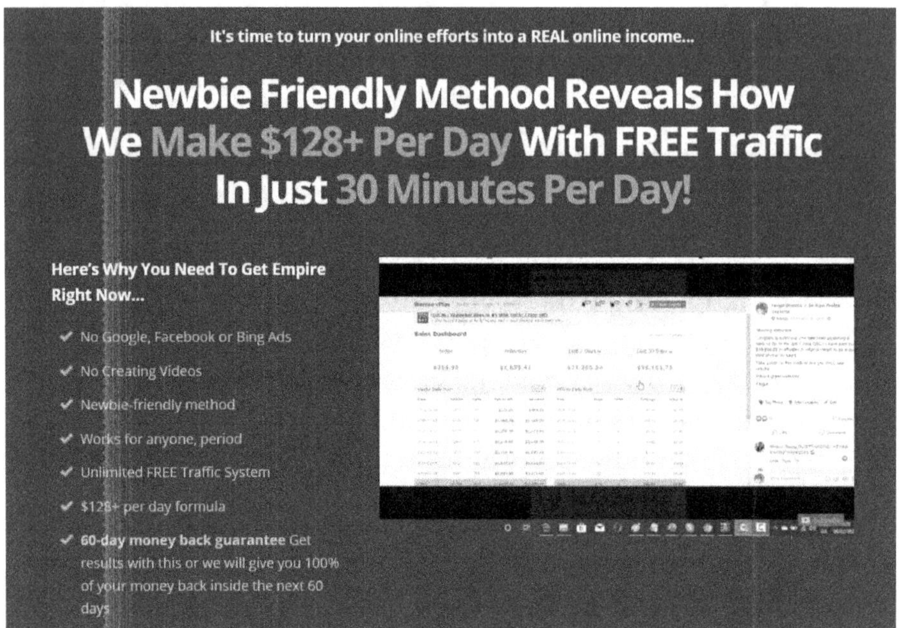

See how the promo uses intro bullets to fight objections and reassure the visitor about their situation and beliefs and tells them how easy the program is, and also states a SOLID Guarantee!

As an exercise, let's take this copy written by Gene Schwartz.

Note down what you think is working for this copy.

How modern Chinese Medicine helps
both men and women

BURN DISEASE
OUT OF YOUR BODY

…lying flat on your back, using nothing
more than the palm of your hand!

This may be the most startling health news you have ever read, dear friend —

And we are going to let you prove its merits to yourself,
without risking a single penny. It is that different. That
powerful. That provocative and controversial.

Let us explain:

THE CHINESE DO NOT BELIEVE IN SURGERY OR MEDICINE FOR
MAJOR ILLNESSES. THEY PREVENT SUCH ILLNESSES INSTEAD—WITH A
SERIES OF MILD, ALMOST EFFORTLESS INTERNAL EXERCISES

If you do not have an open mind, please stop reading here. For this letter is about to introduce you to a new (although it is 4,000 years old), and different type of self healing. Born in China over 40 Centuries ago, it is called Taoist medicine. And we will let the foremost practitioner of it in the Western world—Dr. Stephen T Chang—give you a brief and startling introduction to these effortless exercises.

"Primary symptoms of old age are often experienced as coldness or numbness in the legs and feet due to the deterioration of the circulatory system at the extremities of the body, stiffness of the joints, and the lack of sexual energy. This exercise is designed to reverse these and other degenerative problems of the lower trunk, thus restoring youthfulness to the body."

AND HERE ARE MORE RESULTS DR CHANG PROMISES YOU
—PERHAPS STARTING WITH YOUR VERY FIRST DAY

"Solar plexus exercise." The exercise described in the headline of this letter, in which the Chinese help BURN DISEASE OUT OF THEIR BODIES … lying flat on their back, using nothing more than the palm of their hand. As Dr Chang says, "Building up this fire will help to burn out every disease associated with this area of the body, including diarrhea, constipation, flatulence, diverticulitis, cancer, and other disorders."

"…with consistent practice, the muscles in the abdomen and body will tighten and become toned and strengthened. Excess fat, water and flesh will be eliminated, and the belly will shrink."

"The heart exercise may be practiced morning, noon and night, depending upon the seriousness of the

YOURS TO KEEP FREE—"HOW TO RUB YOUR STOMACH AWAY"…
even if you return "The Complete System of Self-Healing" for every cent of your
purchase price back.

Read full details in enclosed brochure—

You done?

Right, let's compare notes.

Notice how the pre-headline, headline and sub headline draw you into the copy? Further, the headline makes such a bold statement that raises your curiosity… The use of Modern Chinese Medicine lowers skepticism.

With respect to the 1st few paragraphs, can you see how the copy builds immediate kinship with the reader by calling them - 'Dear friend'...

The first paragraph lays the foundation for the copy by telling the reader what they are about to read is going to be shocking and super-controversial. (even more curiosity) ... they don't need to spend a penny (removing the risk and lowering skepticism) ...

Then further validates the reader by asking.... If you do not have an open mind, stop reading here...adds even more credibility to the copy by introducing the Doctor as the foremost practitioner of Chinese Medicine in the world.

Furthermore, the copy introduces the pain points and aggravates the problem but swiftly cuts it short by showing how a "simple" exercise can reverse all the pain and restore youth in the reader.

And finally, it ends with even more risk-reversal and strong bene-fit-driven Guarantee, which backs the solid product!

Important NOTE: This brings us to another point... When we are creating promotions, as said before, we <u>always</u> want only to promote TOP QUALITY PRODUCTS. This applies whether we are building our products or promoting affiliate products, or selling on eBay, Amazon, Fiverr, or wherever.

Yes, it's the purpose of sales copy or promo copy or product reviews to build perceived value so people WILL buy. Still, the actual value of the product must match or preferably exceed the perceived value too!

<u>If your product is NOT up the mark, great promotions like the ones above will no doubt get you sales initially. HOWEVER, buyers will leave unfavorable reviews, and eventually sales will crash. Your personal reputation may take a beating, affecting future promotions.</u>

This is why, towards the beginning of this guide, I mentioned the "Grandma" test…. **If this visitor was my <u>Grandmother</u>, Would I still stand proudly behind my product and sell it to her?**

IN OTHER WORDS, writing good copy is NOT about manipulation. It is about <u>effective communication for a product that your customers will ultimately appreciate</u>!

Here's an example… I recently saw a sales video for a product costing $1500… Despite the price, (and if my wife wouldn't decapitate me), I'd have considered buying it! EXCEPT, one thing held me back (besides the threat of divorce from my wife who thought I was crazy) … The product was about <u>building an email list by a thousand people a day without spending any of your own money</u> (which drew me into a long sales video) … It turned out; you do this by spending several hundred dollars a week on FB Ads and recouping the spent money with an OTO (One Time Offer) and upsells… OK fair enough, BUT one still has to lay out several hundred dollars upfront to "prime the pump" so to speak… In my opinion, I felt a bit duped… "No money spent" apparently meant "Some money spent" (Then the rest of the spending comes out of profits). In other words, I felt I had been "manipulated" into watching this sales video with a false promise… **Therefore, I no longer trusted ANYTHING the sales video said…**

ALWAYS COMMUNICATE THE GENUINE VALUE…. NEVER MANIPULATE!

Consider adding an alternative promo for the same item without the false claim, just to show people how it can be done.

Instead, had the promo said something like "add a thousand people to your email list every day AND get your money back" I would have been a lot more interested in the content.

SOMETHING THAT WILL INCREASE YOUR CONVERSION RATES EVEN WITH MEDIOCRE SALES COPY

What's the ONE thing that can get your product valued highly by prospects? Endorsements by people who have no stake in the success of your sales.

Yep, I'm talking about **testimonials**.

A persuasive copy piece must have three things... An engaging headline, a persuasive opening paragraph, and testimonials! When you can get them, exciting, honest testimonials will significantly boost your sales... The more sincere positive testimonials you have, the better! You can never have "too many" testimonials!

You can get testimonials by...

- Asking your past customers for them.

- Giving out a limited number of your product free in exchange for honest testimonials. If you do this though, make sure to make it absolutely clear that the testimonial has to be genuine and not influenced by the free product. It will also make you look credible if you spell it out that the reviewer got a free sample in exchange for their honest review when you publish the testimonial.

- Copying and pasting positive customer feedback/comments from past sales.

- If you promote an affiliate product, use excerpts of positive reviews from testimonials/product reviews on the product sales page.

The only thing better than blowing your own horn is having other people blowing it for you!

Something Simple and Quick
That Will Instantly Boost Your Sales!

Always have a PS! It is often overlooked, but in any copy, your PS is second in importance to only your headlines! <u>Even if your reader skips the entire body of your copy, statistics show that readers will STILL READ A "PS"!</u> It is an excellent place for you to restate your best benefit, biggest consequence, most exciting bonus, or confirm your no-risk Guarantee!

It's also a great spot to reinforce "scarcity" or "urgency"!

YET ANOTHER POWERFUL WAY TO BUILD EVEN MORE, PERCEIVED VALUE!

In addition to listing the "benefits" of buying your product, list the consequences of not buying your product too! Look at it this way… A potential buyer will take a path of LEAST PAIN. On the one hand, there is the "pain" of parting with DOLLARS, and on the other hand, is the pain of NOT having the product. We must increase the "pain" of NOT buying the product, so it becomes more significant than the "pain" of parting with the money being asked.

People will try to spend their money in a way that brings them the most benefits/pleasure and reduces the most pain. Therefore, the more pleasure (benefits) we can bring to bear if they buy, AND the more PAIN (consequences) we can bring to bear if they do NOT buy, the better chance we have of making a sale!

If you only talk about the "pleasure" of owning a product, you miss half the equation… Talking about the PAIN of NOT owning the product builds perceived value further.

Consequences of NOT buying can include **statements like...**

- "You will continue to struggle to make money."
- "You will remain single."
- "You will kick yourself every time you look at that blank wall."
- "You won't be able to retire."
- "You will forever look at that big hole in your collection."
- "You will regret passing on this offer everytime you slice a tomato."
- "You will continue to take bad pictures."
- "Your family will not be protected"...etc....

An excellent way to clarify the "consequences" of not buying your product is to convert your consequences into questions. This is quite effective because questions "personalize" the consequences for the reader.

- "Do you want to continue struggling to make money?"
- "Do you want to continue to remain single?"
- "Do you want to kick yourself every time you look at that blank wall?"
- "Do you want to be still working at 65+ years of age?"
- "Do you want to continue wasting your money on books that don't work?"
- "Would you rather have less leisure time and more headaches?"

Another way is to just state on the viewer's behalf:

"No, I don't want to grow my email list..."

"No, I don't want to have my family protected..."

etc...

- Something I see often in lead magnet popups

Following any of these "pain" questions with a benefit loaded paragraph would be a very effective way of increasing the perceived value of your product! Sometime back, I saw an AD for a water-filtration system. They stated, "If you buy this filter today, the pain of paying occurs just once; If you DON'T buy, the pain of NOT paying occurs every time you get a glass of water. Which do you want? The 'one-time' pain? Or the 'forever' pain?" I am sure this ad was a massive success!

HOW TO WRITE SO EVEN SKIM READERS ARE DRAWN INTO YOUR SALES COPY AND CONVERTED INTO BUYERS!

TWO kinds of readers will be perusing your offers. "Detail" readers (those who read cover to cover) and "skimmers" (those who just scan your offer). We want to write for BOTH kinds of readers!

One way of getting 'skim readers' to slow down, as was discussed earlier, is to have subtitles / sub-headlines throughout the body of your text to **continually "grab the reader's attention"** and get them to re-engage.

Another way to communicate maximum information to a skin reader is to **use "bullet points."**

- Bullet points break up a long print.
- They also create "white space."

- They eliminate a lot of superfluous words that skim readers hate.

That said, here's a KEY way to tailor our copy to skim readers and detail readers alike. We <u>make use of periodic "highlighting" or "bolding" of parts of the text</u> within the body of our offer. We don't want to overdo it, but a little bolding of key benefits can positively affect our conversion rates.

We want to **bold** or highlight some of the most attractive "benefits" contained within our text copy (just as I bolded key points in the above text!)

Bolded or highlighted text acts much like "mini subtitles," inviting the reader to "engage' in reading the rest of the text!

For example, consider the following 'copy'…

Canon EOS M50 Mirrorless Camera with 15-45 mm Lens Kit 128 GB Full Kit

Capture all your special moments with Canon EOS M50 Mirrorless Camera and cherish the memories over and over again. With 24.1 MP CMOS sensor and AXBA Image processor, this DSLR camera lets you take smooth, detailed, and high-quality images. The 4.2-inch monitor on this Canon 24.1 MP camera makes it easy to view photos, read the menu, and compose shots. With a high ISO sensitivity (up to 17,000), the Canon EOS M50 captures clear images even in low-light conditions. Plus, the 1080p HD movie recording with manual exposure control makes this Canon 24.1 MP camera the right choice for professional photographers. All this considered, this Canon 24.1 MP camera, with an EF-S, IS II 15-45 mm lens, aims to be a great travel companion.

As compared to

Capture all your special moments with **Canon EOS M50 Mirrorless Camera** and cherish the memories over and over again. With 24.1 MP CMOS sensor and AXBA Image processor, this DSLR camera **lets you take smooth, detailed, and high-quality images**. The 4.2-inch monitor on this Canon 24.1 MP camera makes it easy to view photos, read the menu, and compose shots. With a high ISO sensitivity (up to 17,000), the Canon EOS M50 **captures clear photos even in low-light conditions.** Plus, the 1080p HD movie recording with manual exposure control makes this Canon 24.1 MP camera a **good choice for professional photographers**. All this considered, this Canon 24.1 MP camera, with an EF-S, IS II 15-45 mm lens, aims to be a **great travel companion.**

See how, in the second example, the "skim readers" eye is drawn naturally to the key benefits of this camera?

The skim reader sees….

Capture all your special moments with **Canon EOS M50 Mirrorless Camera** and cherish the memories over and over again. With 24.1 MP CMOS sensor and AXBA Image processor, this DSLR camera **lets you take smooth, detailed, and high-quality images**. The 4.2-inch monitor on this Canon 24.1 MP camera makes it easy to view photos, read the menu, and compose shots. With a high ISO sensitivity (up to 17,000), the Canon EOS M50 **captures clear photos even in low-light conditions.** Plus, the 1080p HD movie recording with manual exposure control makes this Canon 24.1 MP camera a **good choice for professional photographers**. All this considered, this Canon 24.1 MP camera, with an EF-S, IS II 15-45 mm lens, aims to be a **great travel companion.**

We can do the same thing with bullet points!

Consider this

Logitech X5000 USB Headset

- Laser-tuned drivers with minimum distortion for crystal clear conversations
- Noise-canceling unidirectional microphone reduces back-

ground noise.
- Optimized for Zoom Conferencing so you can capitalize on conferencing and unified communications
- Padded headband & ear cups with built-in equalizer
- This business product ships in a brown box with no retail packaging

Versus this...

Logitech X5000 USB Headset

- **Laser-tuned drivers** with minimum distortion for **crystal clear conversations**
- Noise-canceling unidirectional microphone **reduces background noise.**
- **Optimized for Zoom Conferencing** so you can <u>capitalize on conferencing</u> and unified communications
- **Padded headband & ear cups** with built-in equalizer
- This business product ships in a brown box with no retail packaging

Again, bolded or highlighted text (used sparingly) can draw attention to your product's most important and best benefits.

The above example also illustrates how the occasional use of <u>underline</u> can work wonders too!

A SUPER SIMPLE WAY TO DIFFERENTIATE YOURSELF FROM THE COMPETITION

Don't Assume Your Customer Knows Anything!

Here's a story I read years back and have retold often, but the lesson is so VALUABLE, it bears repeating...Some decades back, a small beer brewery made beer. They were a tiny brewery with largely unknown brand names. They don't produce a particularly special need... just an average everyday beer...Yet, today, they are a famous top brand!

You know them as **"Coors Beers"**!

As the story goes, one day, an advertising agent was trying to hash out a TV ad 'campaign' for this small unknown company. He asked, **"How do you make your beer?"**. He listened carefully, and then some days later he returned to pitch the TV ad campaign he'd come up with.

The ad started out explaining how at "Coors Beer," they use only the finest purest spring water, quality hops and barley, etc. The commercial went on to say, "Our cookers are precisely temperature and pressure controlled..." etc. etc....

The company owners were unimpressed... They replied, "but EVERY brewery does that!" However, the ad man stood his ground. "**But your CUSTOMERS DON'T KNOW THAT!!!**" The commercials ran, and Coors was transformed into a major brand virtually overnight!

Don't assume your customer knows all of what you do to ensure a high-quality product (or what the creator of an affiliate product does)...

TELL THEM!!

Don't just say; this art piece comes in a matte frame... tell them about how you carefully execute each step to ensure a top-quality matte!

Don't just tell them that the product is "shipped in 48 hours of order placement". Tell them it's packaged in a secure layer of bubble wrap encased in foam within a durable, heavy-duty manila sized double taped envelope!

Don't just tell your blog visitors that this tomato slicer slices tomatoes. Tell them the blades are laser cut for precision and heat-treated for long-lasting sharpness!

The wheels on that office chair are made from a durable polyester plastic of the same type of material used to make bowling balls!

Before endorsing this money-making product, I acquired it and tried it myself to make sure it works. Here's what I did.

Special tip for Amazon and eBay sellers

If you sell on Amazon or eBay, DON'T tell your listing viewers that your product is in pristine condition. Tell them that each 'piece' is also painstakingly inspected before shipment to ensure top quality! It is then secured in a stiff 'no bend' bubble wrap lined envelope to secure it from damage during shipping.

Every eBay or Amazon seller does the above, but YOU'LL be the only one TELLING your customers!

Also, Get Emotional About What Your Product Does!!!

We need to always remember that human beings have "emotional triggers" that will get them to BUY, and we need to tap into these triggers big time.

Has a product ever grabbed your attention, but when you start to read the "copy" it goes on and on about the features of the product and carries no emotion whatsoever ... Result? You get bored, zone out, click off the page...you aren't alone.

Imagine a car advertisement... car driving along a picturesque highway while a voiceover narrates the "easy handling" or "smooth ride"... Yawn!!

Now picture the same car commercial, but the car is now intercut with a roaring fighter jet blasting by... car takes a sharp turn, and the fighter jet does a sharp bank... the car goes up a hill; fighter jet goes into a steep climb.... That communicates "smooth ride / easy handling" in an exciting emotion-packed way!

OR.... A mother drives a car through quiet city streets with a toddler in the rear seat, as the narrator goes on about the gas milea.... BAAAAAM! SMASH!

Cut to a scene showing a smashed vehicle and sound of an ambulance... The final scene is of the mother's quivering hands holding her unharmed child, telling him everything's ALRIGHT as the narrator exclaims, <u>"oh yes, safety side-panel protection with airbags too as nothing is more important than your family"</u>... (if I remember correctly this is a famous Volkswagen ad).

It's common practice for all vehicles to have 'safety side panel protection with airbags,' But THIS advertiser didn't assume people know that, and TOLD people… in a very EMOTIONALLY CAPTIVATING way. **And a feature available in all car brands became a benefit buyers would associate with Volkswagen (only).**

You could even run this ad in a magazine or newspaper or a static webpage using images and still be able to convey the same story and emotion.

AN EASY WAY TO GET READERS TO BELIEVE YOU COMPLETELY

Did you notice how in the previous section, I started with a story? (true story by the way). Often telling an exciting story can 'draw your reader in' and drive a key point (or benefit!) home.

Also, by telling a story, the reader's "skepticism filters" are turned OFF and so you can slide in a lot of benefits without the reader doubting your claims (or at least not nearly as much).

For example, instead of just stating your Guarantee, you might tell how your great grandfather was a woodsmith and how he took such great care of his customers, and how in this day and age that's been lost. That's what inspired you to not only go to such great lengths to ensure a top-quality product and provide the best service possible but also drove you to offer such a comprehensive "no risk" guarantee.

This makes your Guarantee more BELIEVABLE... You know you will honor your Guarantee, but your reader doesn't! Using a story to connect with your reader emotionally, you have instilled a level of solid reassurance for them.

A good story can also trigger the emotions that are so important to motivating buying. For example, instead of just saying, "this book will show you how to make MORE money online", I could recount the story of when my friend suddenly and unexpectedly lost a corporate job due to "restructuring." (again, a true story).

When Sam (my friend), walked into his house "early," his wife knew something was wrong. As he told her the bad news, he could see her fighting back the tears welling in her eyes. Her voice trembling, she asked him how they would manage rent... How would they make the car payment? ... How would they manage to get groceries?... The tragic thing was, he didn't have any answers for her...

That was the day. Sam vowed to himself then and there that he would NEVER become dependent on a "job" again. <u>He also didn't want anyone to go through that pain either</u>. That's why he introduced me to this technique, which I am sharing with you in this book I created.

If you are selling a collectible, you could bring that collectible to life by telling a story of the time from which it came and how people of that era lived.

Imagine reading a story about a person who related how they overheard everyone at the office talking about someone with **bad breath**. Still, she couldn't figure out who they were talking about until she realized it was HER!! (I'll bet you just had an urge to gargle just now... JUST IN CASE!!!)

Do you see how a simple story could turn a boring mouthwash ad into a genuine PANIC ATTACK? Those TV commercials with green cartoon monsters dancing on a cartoon tongue don't get me off the couch, but the thought of ALL MY COWORKERS talking behind my back? Only $29 a bottle? SOLD!!!

Given below is another example of an AD that was used to promote Schlitz Beer.

Study the ad and try to figure out what makes the ad so powerful.

So, why do you think this ad worked so well at converting readers into Schlitz fans?

It immediately arouses curiosity. Secondly, the features and BENEFITS of the offer are revealed as a byproduct of a STORY (conversation between a Doctor and a Nurse), which means the readers 'filters' are not on...

If the headline were to state, "Schlitz Beer Promotes Health..." people would probably scoff it off...

But since the headline starts with 'Why this doctor....' it builds curiosity and also lowers skepticism at the same time.

To sum up, try to think of an emotional story that you can tie into your product offerings. Your prospects will believe in you when they are sufficiently EMOTIONALLY INVESTED in what you have to offer.

HOW TO INCREASE SALES BY OFFERING MORE CHOICES

(And Making Life Easy For Your Customers)

The only 'exit' from your sales page should be the BUY button, if you're selling. Or the signup button, if you're building an email list.

Do one or the other, NOT BOTH AT ONCE!

As a rule, CHOICES will overwhelm your customer and result in INDECISION.

How to turn indecision into an advantage

There are exceptions.... For example, if you have an online store... a "choice" can be a way of offering an upsell or deluxe version of your product.

But that's not a real "multiple choice" because, in most cases, the products are offered one at a time with the upsell coming AFTER the buyer has bought the main product.

Another example of a *"choice that isn't a true choice"* is where one has a sales page with an exit script to capture email addresses… Same principle… <u>The "choice" is offered only AFTER the prospect has decided on the 1st offer (the sales page offer</u> - in this case, upon not buying and exiting the sale page, they are presented with a 2nd SEPARATE offer).

When a TRUE "choice" is being offered, it is often because it is being used to psychological effect to build the "perceived value" of the offer (NOTE: As said, "Perceived Value" is simply the value your prospect feels your offer has) …. Here's an example of using 'choice' to build "perceived value"…

Suppose we offer a **WordPress Plugin** that does something wonderful for WordPress Sites (it doesn't matter what) …And we close with this buy button….

We might make a sale… Is there a way we can increase the customer's "perceived value" of our plugin by offering a "choice"?

YES! Our brains are poor at estimating "absolute" VALUE but excellent at making "comparison" VALUES. So… Suppose we offered this instead…

Most buyers will be driven towards the middle price… Here's how psychology is working … "OK at $17 it's a no brainer decision … but wait … for just $10 more I can do unlimited personal sites! So, the middle option beats out the left option. <u>The ADDED perceived value here is the number of sites we can use this plugin on.</u>

That "comparison" just wasn't shown with the single buy button… With the single buy button, we may feel like the price is high, but **by offering the "choice," the higher price shows as a bargain!**

In the 1st case, our brains are poor at telling us if the plugin is worth $27 with no alternative to compare it to, but in the 2nd case, our brain is GREAT at telling us the $27 deal is much better than the $17 deal! (Note: That our brain is excellent at making "comparisons" is another reason why the "apples to oranges" strategy, covered earlier, works so well!).

Similarly, the $70 jump from the middle offer to the right-hand offer enhances the middle offer's perceived value again! The vast majority of buyers are likely not planning on doing "client" sites, and so the middle offer stands out nicely!

For the few doing (or planning to do) client sites, the $70 difference is nothing compared to what they can earn just doing 1 - 2 client sites.

The "choice" here isn't really a choice as much as it's a way to BUILD VALUE!

Another way to use "choice" as a way of increasing perceived value is to offer a much lower quality alternative for a NOT very much cheaper price than a deluxe product... For example, suppose you had a product called **22 Unique Ways Guaranteed To Get You Free Targeted Traffic** priced at **$27**... How can we use "choice" to increase the perceived value of the product? SIMPLE...Our brains are relatively poor at determining "absolute value" but excellent at determining "relative value" ... SO....

Try breaking your offer into two products...
- **6 Unique Ways To Get Free Targeted Traffic - $24.50**
- **22 Unique Ways to Get Free Targeted Traffic - $27**

For just $2.50 more, they get 16 more ways! We don't really expect anyone to take the 'cheaper' deal, but it sure adds perceived value to the deluxe product!

BONUS SECTION

HOW TO POWERFULLY TAP INTO PEOPLE'S EMOTIONAL BUYING TRIGGERS

As I've been saying time and again, the BIGGEST thing to realize about people is that they buy based on EMO-TION!!! This section shows you how to access deeper and stronger, stronger emotions in your prospects to motivate them to take action and BUY!

First, we need to realize that although people like to appear 'logical' in their buying decisions (often they will recite whole lists of 'logical reasons' why they bought something), <u>the actual decision to buy is always based on emotion.</u>

It is often said by sales professionals and copywriting experts, that people are 90% emotional and 10% logical in their buying decisions. I like to go one step further and say that people buy on **ONE HUNDRED PERCENT** emotion and then use "logic" to HIDE their true buying motivations.

Either way, we need to always remember that human beings have STRONG "emotional triggers" that will get them to BUY if we can tap into them.

So many times, I come across an exciting product with a dull copy that bores the life out of me talking emotionlessly about its features...I get bored...zone out...and click out!

AS AN EXAMPLE, <u>picture trying to write a sales piece for an emergency gas-powered generator...</u> Before you started reading this book, you might have been tempted to say, Oh, this generator generates X amps and Y volts for Z hours... and these would be good features to list BUT... Now you're smarter...you know you need to list BENEFITS... Be ready for the next Katrina (hurricane)...It's not a question of "if" but of "when"... And again, this is on the right track, but we can do better....

How's this for an emotion-packed headline...

<u>"Daddy, I'm Cold and 'Fraid Of The Dark"</u>
That's What My Shivering 4-Year-Old Daughter
Said To Me When A Winter Storm Knocked Out
Our Power In The Middle Of The Night

Emotion packed headline without even mentioning the product!!

Suddenly we're not appealing to the 'logical' portion of the brain that says, "What are the odds of a severe storm, etc."

We are focusing on EMOTION..."I will do ANYTHING to protect

my family!!!"

Plus, we're now "invested" in the father's dilemma! How does he solve this and comfort his frightened, cold daughter? <u>We're almost FORCED to read on!</u>

Common Emotional Triggers include…

- Money / Financial Security
- Health
- Sex / Companionship
- Approval of Others
- Safety
- Taking Care of Family
- Avoiding Embarrassment
- Self-Indulgence / Reward
- Have More Time To Do The Things We Enjoy
- Etc.…

One of your Bonuses for this book is titled "Emotional Power Words." You can use it as a swipe file to insert more emotion into your offers.

Other Psychological Factors You Need To Be Aware of And Use in Your Offers Follow:

In addition to realizing that people always buy based on emotion and that we need to activate their emotional triggers to get them to buy, there are some other human decision-making psychological factors we must be aware of.…

WIIFM

The first is that people act out of their self-interest…The so-called WIIFM (What's in it for me?).

Your offer MUST answer this question explicitly. Don't leave it to be guessed by the reader.

And, ensure your benefits make sense.

Look at the following sales copy (I have removed the product name and the author name in this critique) ...

"Discover How To Use ▇▇▇▇ In Your Marketing To Get More Attention, Generate More Leads And Make More Sales"

These Tips Will Help You To Improve Your Social Media Marketing And Show You How To Better Connect With Your Customers

Operating and growing as a work-from-home entrepreneur takes some severe self-discipline.

While any business is going to take a considerable amount of marketing to get off the ground, starting a business on a budget limits your options.

That's why a lot of business owners turn to free channels such as social media.

But they often ignore ▇▇▇▇

Which is crazy, because it's a great way to have personal customer contact.

▇▇▇▇ For Marketing

▇▇▇ is one of the best ways any business owner is going to have to connect personally with their customer base. Not many other options allow you to get into your customers' hands and have them take a physical action to see your messages.

That small step can increase conversions by making it seem voluntary for your customers to see your message.

As An Entrepreneur, You Need To Connect

Maybe it's just me, but I see no clear BENEFIT(S) here. No emotions are triggered. The second sentence in the first paragraph under the **"For Marketing,"** sub headline doesn't even make any sense. - " Not many other options allow you to get into your customers' hands and have them take a physical action to see your messages."

And... the sub-headline conveys features, but NO BENEFIT!!!

The message above doesn't make abundantly clear WIIFM (What's In It For Me?)

Don't expect your prospects to ask.

Here's another issue… The opening paragraph is a series of negative points about owning an online business…

- It takes some serious self-discipline.
- It takes a huge amount of marketing to get off the ground.
- Starting a business on a budget limits your options.

Gee! If I wasn't already overwhelmed, I sure am now! Only state negatives in terms of how your product SOLVES or ELIMINATES them.

Let's do a quick fix-up of this copy by creating a "USP first" headline, adding in some benefits & emotional triggers, and adding in some power words too.

WARNING: If Your Business Already Has Too Many Customers, This Book Is Not for You

Discover How You Can EASILY Generate Tons More Leads, Sales & Income at Will Using A Secret Simple To Use FREE Social Site (And Build A Business You'll Be PROUD OF!)

97% Of Marketers Either Don't Know This Special Site Exists, Or They Are Using It Wrong And Leaving PILES OF MONEY On The Table!

Want A Simple Step by Step Social Marketing Plan (Using This 'Secret Site') That WORKS For ANY Business And Takes ZERO DOLLARS and Very Little Time To Implement?

Want To Instantly Tap Into The Power of Social Marketing With ZERO Tech Skills Needed?

Tired of Being A 'Slave' To Your Business? Want Higher Profits With Less Work?

Want A Profitable Business Plan GUARANTEED To Work Or Your Money Back?

At Last, The World Is Your Oyster! You Can NOW Build Your Online Business On YOUR OWN TERMS on YOUR OWN SCHEDULE!

Building relationships with your new and existing customers is one of the best ways any business can explode their sales and differentiate themselves from the competition.

But who has time to connect personally with everybody in their customer base? There are not many options out there that aren't costly and a lot of work, BUT FORTUNATELY, there is one FREE solution that is efficient and so allows you more free leisure time to enjoy your profits!

HERE'S THE SECRET… When your customers feel they are seeing your messages "voluntarily," they are much more open to what you have to offer! That translates to MORE SALES and MUCH HIGHER PROFITS for YOU!

As an entrepreneur, the opportunity to connect efficiently with your audience is an amazing one.

This secret social site (revealed in the book below) allows you to ask your customers questions and figure out what problems they have. As a result, you can market to them on a very customized and personal level and be light years about your competition)

With more time, we could do better, but that's just off the top of my head... We now have a much more BENEFITS driven promo, and we are using power words such as FREE, EASY, SIMPLE, etc. We don't have 'higher profits,' we have 'MUCH higher profits.' We don't have 'more time,' we have 'more LEISURE time'... etc.

We've coupled every feature with one or more BENEFITS (later, we would get into the consequences of passing on the offer, such as - Do you want to continue beating your head against the wall with endless hours of work for little or no results? Or would you rather have great results, lots more leisure time, and no more headaches?)

Most importantly, we've injected some EMOTION into the copy, and with all the benefits and emotional triggers, the reader is more "invested" in the copy and driven to read more... Remember that customers want MORE for LESS, FASTER, and EASIER. Hit all those triggers if you can... REPEATEDLY!!

We've also used highlighting for skim readers...

In a nutshell, we've made it clear WIIFM.

Now, let me introduce you to the concept of FIGS.

FIGS: This stands for:
- **F**ear of Loss
- **I**mmediate Gratification
- **G**reed
- **S**ense of Urgency

The more of these attributes you can incorporate into your offer, the higher your conversions will be.

Let's talk about them in reverse order...

<u>Sense Of Urgency</u> - It's human nature to put off making a decision for as long as possible. If a person can 'put off' making a decision, they will.... And they will go for as long as they can get away with

NOT making a decision. SO… We always need to create a sense of urgency in our offers! There are several ways to do this, including…

- Giving a warning that the price will increase shortly
- Letting people know the offer may be withdrawn at any time
- Offering an "early bird" bonus (1st 100 buyers for example)
- Get in on the ground floor.
- Etc…

Given below is a Classic example of URGENCY used in advertising. The US Army ran this AD in 1967.

The image of the young boy looking SUPER-UPSET while staring at a piece of paper in his hand just adds to the curiosity element.

If the AD said, "Here is how to join the Army," even if someone did want to apply, they would probably put it off for later, because - What's the hurry?

But instead, the AD states that this young man has already lost his chance to make a choice, and opportunity is slim… so if you don't want to end up like him (i.e., without a choice)….CURIOSITY + URGENCY … you should act now and apply for the Army to get your choice of rank.

This line defines the advertisement in a nutshell. **"Hey, you could have joined early and become a combat engineer or some such; now you're infantry."**

Always create URGENCY in your offers.

Greed - People always want MORE!!! That's OK...In fact, that's excellent! Here are ways we can offer "more" to our customers…

We can offer…
- Bonuses
- Bonus chapters
- Worksheets
- FREE Resource Links
- FREE Support
- Lifetime Free Updates
- Case Studies
- FREE membership in a closed FB group/forum

I had a client who put together a great book (pdf) but had no bonuses… I advised him to break the pdf into parts and call the 2nd part a BONUS. The result? Much higher PERCEIVED VALUE and more sales!

Immediate Gratification - We live in an "instant" world. People want gratification ASAP! Look at how much Amazon invests in making sure people know how quickly they will get their stuff shipped. Look at the BILLIONS of dollars Amazon has made on their PRIME service, which offers faster shipping…

Look at diet commercials that stress how much weight was lost in the 1st week… Or recipe books that feature FAST recipes… People want their promised benefits as soon as possible!

We can highlight this "instant gratification" in several ways.

- You can give people instant access/download - Even if we are selling a physical product if we can offer a bonus digital download, that constitutes instant gratification…

NOTE: Even buy buttons can build perceived value by creating urgency and <u>instant gratification.</u>

The "TODAY's SPECIAL" creates urgency because people aren't sure when the price may go up.

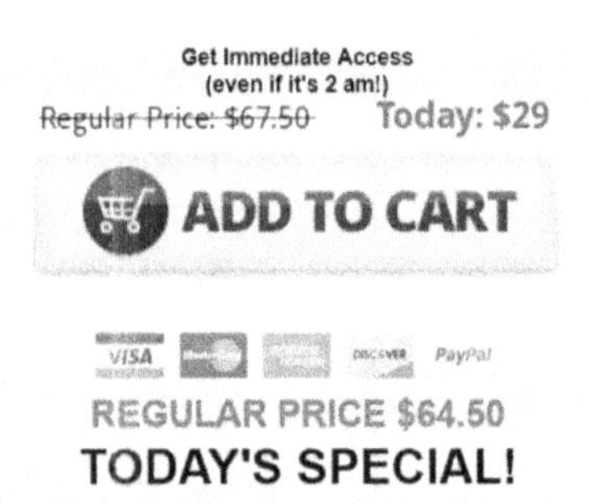

The "Get Immediate Access (even if it's 2 am!)" explicitly reinforces the instant gratification (don't assume your customer KNOWS it's an instant download!)

You can also feed the instant gratification desire...

- By listing the shipping time if it's a physical product.
- When describing the product. Stress the quick/fast/instant results.

<u>Fear of Loss</u> - This is similar to a "sense of urgency" but deals with "limited supply." Whereas "Price going up soon" is a 'sense of urgency' phrase, "only 50 will be sold" is a 'fear of loss' phrase... People fear that if they don't buy now, they will LOSE the option...

Here are some ways we can highlight 'fear of loss'....
- "Limited Supply - Once sold out, they are gone."
- "Only _______ will be sold!"
- "Limited Collector's Edition"

We can also go after 'fear of loss' in what the product offers...

- "Get your hands on this before your competition does!"
- "Get this home business tax guide before the IRS comes knocking at your door!"

That said, the BIGGEST, yet simplest 'fear of loss' is just to tell people the CONSEQUENCES of NOT having your product as previously discussed.

- You can continue to struggle to make money.
- You can continue to spend Saturday nights single and home alone.

- Without this hose, you can blindly HOPE the fire department gets there before your home with all your belongings burns to the ground.

A SIMPLE TIP TO INCREASE SALES

- "Reassure" Your Reader!

Here is an oft' overlooked tip - ALWAYS remember to RE-ASSURE YOUR READER! This applies both in your sales copy and your actual product (if it's a written product or has instructions).

People don't like to admit it but generally speaking, they are insecure and afraid of failure... They may want to try our product, but they are scared they are going to screw something up, so they hesitate... People HATE getting out of their comfort zones. We need to take them by the hand (figuratively) and reassure them they can do this, benefit from this, operate this product, execute this tutorial or what have you...

Remember way back at the intro to this guide when I went over what's included in this book? When I mentioned the "psychology of buying," <u>I immediately followed that with a "Don't worry, it's simple stuff"</u> ... That's because "buying psychology" sounds ominous. It was important for me to clarify that wouldn't be the case here, as I have only introduced those elements that are necessary AND reduced them into digestible, bite-sized pieces.

Often in sales copy, if I describe a feature or benefit that sounds complicated (but isn't), I might say something like …

- And this is so simple even a complete newbie can do it.
- And when you see how, you'll slap yourself at how simple it is!
- Don't worry. I include easy to follow step-by-step instructions with clear screenshots.
- It's like - looking over my shoulder as I show you exactly how to do it.
- Don't worry. It's not complicated at all. I take you by the hand and lead you through every step of the process.

NOTE: Your GUARANTEE is a great place to reassure your customer!!

HOW TO ADAPT YOUR COPY FOR EMAIL, SOCIAL MEDIA POSTS, PRODUCT REVIEW PAGES, AND SELF-PUBLISHED AMAZON BOOKS

So far, we've concentrated on creating persuasive promos for sales pages. NOW we will discuss how to modify things for special situations…. Email promos, product review pages, and self-published book descriptions. This will allow you to get the maximum response and conversions from these types of offers.

Email Promos:

The thing that makes email promos different is that you have a personal relationship built with your subscribers (or should have!). As such, you have to present your email offers as if you were making a recommendation to a friend. In fact, that's a good guideline for ANY promo. If you wouldn't offer it to a friend, you shouldn't be offering it at all.

Also, with emails, every email should NOT be a promo. When emailing a list of subscribers, you will have TWO types of emails going out… Relationship building emails (where you aren't selling anything but offering free tips, resources, or help) and Promotion emails that offer quality affiliate products, your own products… Etc.

Try and keep to a 50/50 mix… Also, email often. Your subscribers will be quick to forget who you are if you don't email on at least a semi-regular basis… If you provide VALUE and give what your subscribers want, they won't mind hearing from you often and will grow to trust your product recommendations.

The KEY to successfully promoting an affiliate product via email is to start by giving an HONEST appraisal/review of said product (same applies for product review pages too!)

An email product promo that extols nothing but POSITIVE things about the product will often be met with skepticism by subscribers; however, if you state 1 or 2 negatives also, that **creates instant credibility** for you because your review comes across as honest and objective. I like to sandwich a negative between two positives.

TIP: How can you use a negative product feature to skyrocket your sales?

Here's what you do… create a bonus that overcomes the shortcoming and offer it as an exclusive bonus to anyone who buys the affiliate product through your link!

For example, suppose we're promoting a product that shows people how to make money creating YouTube videos, but one negative is the product doesn't go into a lot of details on how to create the videos. We could put together a tutorial on how to do that with free software... It needn't be very extensive; even links to existing online tutorials will suffice. The point is to help the prospect use the product better....

Then in your email promo, you might say something like...

"This product provides a step-by-step newbie friendly way anyone can make $55 - $342 per short video they create on YT.

The only slight downside is the book assumes you know how to upload videos. However, I have fixed this for you...

When you purchase through my link, I include my exclusive bonus that shows you how to create videos using FREE simple to use software and how to efficiently upload your high-profit creations to YT.... so, you're covered".

There. You have a negative sandwiched between two positives, and one positive is a great exclusive bonus! Now, if you didn't want to create this bonus (perhaps you already have a different bonus), you could say:

"This product provides a step-by-step newbie friendly way anyone can make $55-$342 per short video they create on YT.

The only slight downside is the book assumes you know how to make and upload videos. However, this turned out to NOT be a big deal as you would think.

It turns out, you can use a simple FREE software program called CamShot to make your short videos, and there are lots of tutorials on how to use this software. I have included a list of all freely available videos that will get you up to speed with CamShot.

Again, we have a negative sandwiched between two positives where the second positive is a FIX of the negative!

The final point with email is your **email subject line**. This is an important part of your email because it determines whether your email gets opened!

Generally speaking, your email subject line needs to…
- Let your subscribers know it's you.
- Be specific as to what's inside.
- Be of such value to your subscribers that they want to open your email immediately.

Some subscribers will open your email simply because it is from you, and they like you that much and look forward to your emails. For example, all of your email subject lines can begin with "[Your Name] Tips" or "[Your Name] Free Tips."

Some will open your emails because the subject line promises something specific and exciting that they WANT.

Examples: "High-Profit Amazon Books in 1-2 Hours is LIVE!

"INSTANTLY Double or TRIPLE Your Affiliate Commissions??"

"Easy Way To Get BUYER Traffic To Your Funnel Or Offer FAST"

Some will open your emails because the subject line is arousing curiosity!

Examples: "Have You Ever Had Brain Surgery While Conscious?"

"How Many Publishers Does It Take To Screw In A Light Bulb?"

"It's Like Legally Printing Money…"

Email subject lines that offer a general benefit without getting into anything specific stand a much lower chance of being opened because they just blend into all the background noise. For example, what would you open first (if, at all)?

SUBJ: Make More Money Now! Simple Method!
SUBJ: Make $1247 From One FB Post? Here's How…

See how the 1st Subject line is so non-specific we tend to dismiss it? I don't have time to open every email out there, promising me "more money"... I need specifics.

On the other hand, the 2nd Subject line is quite specific... A $1247 from one FB post, and here's how to do it... Curiosity alone would get me to open this one...

This 2nd subject line also uses another subtle psychological technique to bypass skepticism, which you should recognize by now (you do right?). If you said it states the benefit in the form of a question, pat yourself on the back.

Again, by doing this, we do not ask the reader to accept a claim but rather consider if something is possible... The latter is met with more of an open mind.

For example, If I said to you, "I can jump off the roof of my house and not injure myself" .... You'd be like Ya right buddy as you started dialing 911.

BUT... If I said... "Hey ... Do you think I could jump off the roof of my house without injuring myself?", you might say, Well, I don't think so, but what makes you think you can?? ... Suddenly you are more open-minded to the possibility...

Product Review Pages:

A product review page works much like an email promo... You build credibility by including one or two negatives about the product. As long as you can also cite 'fixes' for them in your review, you are OK. For example, perhaps the negative is that the user manual isn't user friendly, BUT you include some links to other online tutorials that are more user friendly.

The main difference between a review page (or an email promo) and a sales page is, the review page doesn't sell, it "presents"... It's up to the actual sales page (you send the reader to) to "sell" the product... Your affiliate promo is only meant to put the reader in a positive pre-frame (mood) about the product.

By reviewing a product in an informative way, you <u>empower your prospect</u>, so they feel <u>confident when they click through to and read the actual sales page</u>… You've warned them of minefields to look out for and revealed to them the good points of the product and <u>gotten them emotionally excited about what this item can do for them!</u>

Writing Enticing Descriptions For Self-Published Books

If you are a self-publisher (or plan to be), remember that the purpose of your book description is to get people to BUY the book! We do this by…

1. **Tapping into our reader's EMOTIONS -** What is it about our book that will trigger excitement in our reader's mind?

2. **Making the BENEFITS of our book clear** (i.e., what problem will the book solve? Or What pleasure will it bring?)

Here are some further tips if you self-publish or plan to self-publish books on Amazon:

- There are TWO descriptions… One that appears on your book itself, and the other that appears on Amazon listing… the description on the Amazon listing should be as long as possible as the longer people spend viewing your Amazon listing, the better Amazon ranks your book!

- Of course, BOTH Descriptions should entice the reader and make them want to BUY your book as per their new found knowledge.

Social Media Promos

Social Media promos are very different from the traditional copy that we write for websites, emails, etc.

In a social media promo, you need to come up with a **wholly unrelated BUT interesting story** <u>that eventually ties in with the product being offered</u>.

Conversations are already taking place in social media. You need to find a way to enter those conversations and MAKE THE SHIFT in your prospect's head that is necessary for you to exchange value with them.

Another reason Social Media promos are different is you aren't writing for one specific person. It would be best if you cast a wider net.

For example - It doesn't matter if you are 22 or 52. This regime can help you shed 30 lbs in 90 days!

Let's take a look at some successful Social Media Posts:

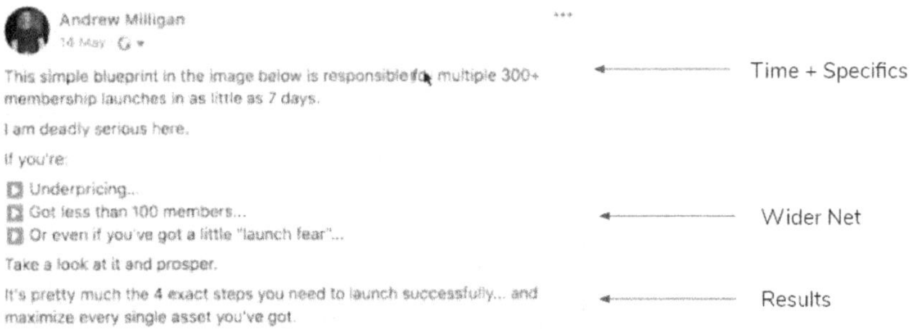

See how Andrew dishes out very lucrative specifics (multiple 300+ memberships), reaches out to a wider group of readers, validates them (by casting a wide net), and dangles a mouth-watering result in front of them?

The reader isn't just in for a big break; they stand to lose out on all those benefits if they don't read what Andrew has to say.

Take a look at another Facebook promo written by yours truly.

Note how this post transitions into a sales message.

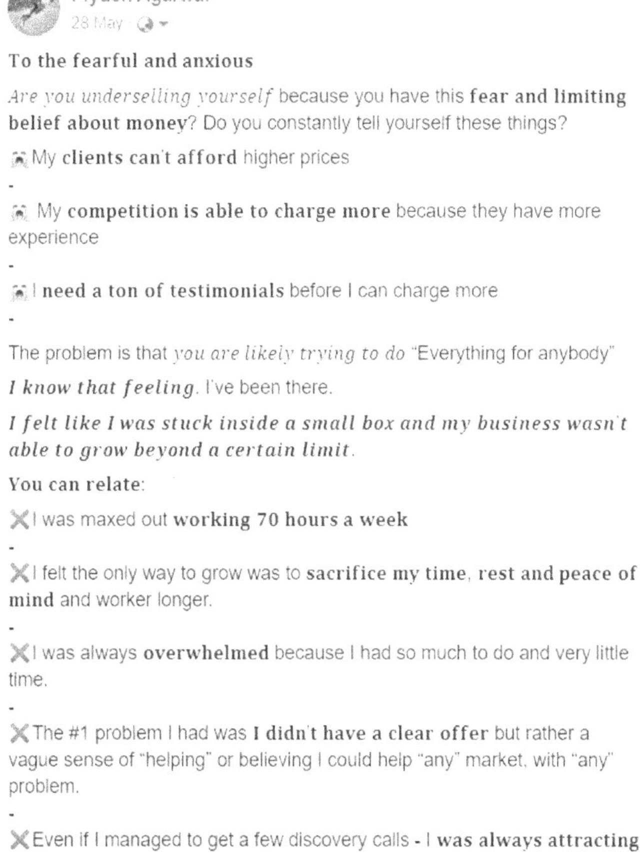

The image above is incomplete. You can read the full post here. https://www.facebook.com/piyushbiz/ videos/145551917094182/

As you can see, the post starts with a compelling hook., "To the Fearful and Anxious…".. This is guaranteed to arrest attention and make the reader curious about what I am about to say, as most of my prospects are - Fearful and anxious about their present situation.

Next, it validates the beliefs and frustrations of the reader by casting a wider net by re-asserting their problems - are they stuck with low paying clients? Are they underselling themselves... Etc..

And then transitions the story by talking about the author's problems by mirroring the prospect's beliefs, frustrations, fears, and objections.

By recalling a similar situation from their own life, the writer bonds with the reader.

Then introduces the significant benefit - the reader can leverage the writer's experience to learn how to get high-paying clients. The value proposition is raised so high that opting into the offer becomes a no-brainer for the reader.

FROM BLANK PAGE TO COMPLETED PROMO CREATING HYPNOTIC OFFERS STEP-BY-STEP

Summary

Well, we've come a long way, haven't we? I'm sure you're feeling a bit overwhelmed... maybe a lot overwhelmed... DON'T WORRY. The GOOD NEWS IS, you don't have to use every idea in this guide to be successful at writing powerfully hypnotic offers! This book was written as a reference you could go back to again and again and again as needed. Start with the basics and build.

As long as you remember that although features are good, it's the **BENEFITS THAT SELL** you are off to a great start. You are avoiding the number one mistake I see inexperienced (and even experienced!!) copywriters make... neglecting BENEFITS!

It's great that the hose sprays to roof level at 8gpm (feature), but its ability to extinguish a house fire before the fire department gets there is the BENEFIT!

Next, remember that people buy on EMOTION… **Keep your benefits as emotionally charged as possible, and you'll get sales!**

- Can you imagine how embarrassed I was when…?
- I was so proud when…
- I couldn't believe the peace of mind that came with not having to live paycheck to paycheck.
- The happy look on my child's face was priceless….

Part of being able to hit your customers' emotion 'hot spots' or 'triggers' lies in **KNOWING your typical customer and their beliefs and echoing and VALIDATING those beliefs**…. This is how we emotionally connect with your customers and form a kinship with them! Also, **REASSURE** your customers! **Example…**

If You've Dreamed Of The Day, You Could Tell Google To Take A Hike. Your Dream Is About To Come True!

Have you been trying to rank on Google and failed? If so, it's NOT your fault! <u>Even SEO experts are losing ground because Google keeps changing the rules</u>!

Finally, before you start, decide on what your USP will be… What will be your **Unique Selling Position** (your unique vision) that will get people to buy off of YOU rather than anyone else?

For example, the USP for this book is it's more than just a book about copywriting…. It delves into buyer psychology and what makes people BUY.

In Summarizing, we see that a good piece of copy has the following components…

Pre-headline, Headline, Sub headline - These headlines draw the reader into the copy. Your headlines can…

- State your main benefit in an emotional way
- Make a PROMISE that draws the reader in, or...
- Arouse curiosity that COMPELS the reader to read on

Opening Paragraph - This is the most important paragraph of the entire sales or promo page. <u>It expands on the main benefit</u> and <u>draws the reader into the rest of the copy</u>. Be sure this paragraph hits those emotional triggers!

The Body - Reveals additional features coupled with <u>benefits</u>, <u>benefits</u>, and <u>more benefits</u>. We try to include as many emotional triggers within our text as possible.

Better yet, <u>include a story</u> that causes the reader to emotionally invest in our offer (we also include "consequences" of NOT getting our product!)

Additional Headlines Within The Body - Additional headlines within the body of our sales letter, product review, or Promotion (or listing) create "white space" for a more pleasant look and also make the promo easier to read.

It also continually gets the skim reader to "re-engage" into the body text. **BOLDED** or <u>Underlined</u> or Highlighted text (used sparingly) can also get "skim readers" to slow down and "(re)engage" with the copy.

A Great Looking Opening Image / Video (& Lots Of Additional Images) taps into the emotional triggers of the reader. It creates a visual representation of the product and product claims. <u>Images visually reinforce the claims in print, which is psychologically compelling</u>.

Testimonials - Don't forget this component! It's crucial and powerful.

Strong Guarantee - A strong guarantee removes all the risk for your buyer. <u>It's also a great opportunity to REASSURE your buyer</u>. ALSO, a well-stated guarantee can make your customer feel good and feel SPECIAL, and so it is a great "bonding" opportunity too.

Call(s) to Action - Don't assume readers will click. TELL THEM exactly what to do. Always have repeated calls to action! Say things like...

"Don't lose your chance to own this course! Click The BUY Button Now!"
"Click the BUY NOW Button to Lock in Your Special Price"
"Click Here Now for Complete Info" Etc...

Don't forget to create "urgency' and "scarcity" and tell your customer EVERYTHING you do to ensure a great quality product and great service!

I usually have at least <u>THREE</u> calls to action (sometimes more).... One near the beginning of my copy, right after my opening and first few paragraphs, or bullet points and/or after a picture of the product <u>with a buy button</u>... Then after my complete product description, another stronger CTA and buy button, following that with a "WAIT, There's MORE!!" and I introduce the bonuses with a strong CTA/Buy button. Finally, I summarize everything the buyer gets with a compelling call to action at the end.

A PS - Next to the headline, this is the most commonly read part of the copy. Take advantage of the PS to restate your best benefit, restate your Guarantee, remind people that the price is going up, etc. <u>Your PS should contain yet another stronger Call to Action.</u>

HERE'S HOW I GO FROM A BLANK PAGE TO A COMPLETED WRITTEN PROMO

When preparing a promotion, here are the specific steps I go through....

STEP 1 - Research The Product - For example, If I were reviewing an affiliate product, I would review the product's sales page and learn all I can about the product. If the reviews are available, I would look at them.

If I were listing a product on Amazon, I would look at similar product listings on Amazon. Look at listing descriptions and also look at reviews. I want to see what people are liking and disliking and what they consider important.

STEP 2 - Research My Typical Customers - You'll already have a pretty good idea of what your typical customers like from the previous step, but you may be able to expand on this by searching and visiting forums, FB groups, and pages, etc.

Step 3 - Define My USP (Vision) - Now, I either deduce the product creator's USP or create my OWN USP for the product. If it's an affiliate product, my USP is often my exclusive bonus!

Step 4 - List Features & Tons of Benefits - Next, I start writing down EVERY SINGLE PRODUCT FEATURE AND BENEFIT I can think of... <u>Are there any benefits the product creator hasn't thought of?</u> I go back through the list... <u>Are there any features I wrote that don't have a corresponding benefit?</u> If so, I add the benefit(s) to that feature. I may start to add in "power words" at this point, but if not, that's OK - we can add them later... (look at competing products to generate swipe files)

I go through the list again, and this time I'm looking to <u>put the benefits into emotional terms</u>.... For example, your thought process might go something like this...

- **FEATURE** - "teach your dog not to bark" ...

- **ADD POWER WORDS** - "Easily Teach Your Dog Not to Bark in Just 7 Days"

- **FEATURE WITH BENEFIT** - "Finally Get A Full Night's Sleep! - Easily Teach Your Dog Not To Bark in 7 Days!"

- **FEATURE WITH EMOTIONAL BENEFIT** - "Finally Get A Full Night's Sleep! Easily Teach Your Best Friend Not TO Bark in Just 7 Days1"

Step 5 - Start Working On Headlines - Use your <u>strongest benefit</u>, use power words, trigger powerful emotions, arouse curiosity, offer a promise.

I usually end up creating many headlines and re-writing them to get them better and better. Time spent on creating a good powerful headline is ALWAYS time well spent as this is the most important part of your promo... It determines if your email gets opened, if your listing gets clicked on, or if your sales page/product review page gets read.

I usually end up with a handful of great headlines… I pick the best, and that becomes my main headline… You can then flesh it out further by adding a pre-headline and sub-headline if you wish. I usually then use my other good headlines as subheadings within my promo to keep the reader engaged, as previously discussed.

Step 6 - Write Opening Paragraph - It expands on my headline, and <u>piles on the benefits, so the reader is enticed to keep reading</u>. Your opening paragraph is also the place to get your USP out (remember to lead with your USP, not your product) and form a kinship or emotional BOND with your customer. Your opening paragraph is a great place to insert a hook such as "see the excellent bonuses included below?" or "by the end of this page you'll know how to…".

DON'T FORGET that opening with an interesting STORY can be one of the best ways to use your opening paragraph to BOND and emotionally connect with your reader, get them "invested" in your copy, and get the emotional benefits communicated with the least skepticism.

Next, the rest of the body just flows as the sub-headlines outline the points (benefits) I'm covering. You might change the order of the sub-headlines as needed (remember to compare "apples to oranges"!)

Step 7 - Go Back And Add-In More Power Words, More Emotion, and Add-in More Emotional Images Too If You Can - Add in the additional copy for your bonuses (if applicable). Go back and insert the negative consequences of NOT getting the product!

Step 8 - Go In And Insert Your Testimonials, Guarantee, And Calls To Action - Make sure the Guarantee makes your customer feel very reassured and special too. Make sure your calls to action create a sense of urgency.

Step 9 - Conclude With Your PS - Decide what you want to re-stress.

TIP: You can even have multiple PS's as in PS, PPS, PPPS…. Restate the Guarantee, restate when the price is going up, and then do an "apples to oranges" price comparison with the final call to action.

Step 10 - FINALLY, Do A Very Thorough Spelling / Grammar Check - Spelling errors won't absolutely "kill" your sales, but it will eat away at them. [OPTIONAL] If time permits, put your promo away for a couple of days and come back later with fresh eyes and see if you can improve it (HINT: Trust me, you can AL-WAYS improve it!)

In the end, don't expect perfection! If we as marketers demanded perfection from ourselves, we'd never get any promotions out there!

At some point, you have to say "good enough" and move on to the next promo. You'll get better with each project, but if you've read through this book and bonuses, at least now you won't completely blow it when you do a promo, listing, product review, email broadcast, or social media post.

Don't be afraid to refer back to this guide often and as needed! **You have the benefit of 10+ years of expert experience packed into about X info-packed pages….** Make things easy on yourself and REVIEW the promo secrets in this guide regularly!

All the best!

Your "Hypnotic Offer" Buddy,

Piyush